Building services design

Thomas W. Maver BSc, PhD

Building services design

a systemic approach to decision-making

RIBA Publications Limited

First published 1971

© Thomas W. Maver 1971

Designed and published by
RIBA Publications Limited
66 Portland Place, London WIN 4AD

Illustrations drawn by
Laing Livesey Partners

Printed in Great Britain by
Alden & Mowbray Ltd, Oxford

Erratum
Figure 2.7 (page 32) should be number 2.9. Figure 2.9 (page 37) should be number 2.10. The correct figure 2.7 is reproduced below, having been omitted from the original text. Figures 2.9, 2.10 are also reproduced on this sheet for your convenience.

Figure 2.7

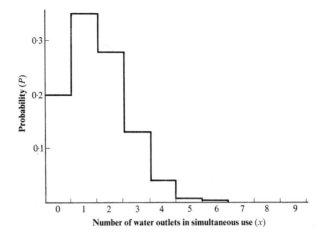

Number of water outlets in simultaneous use (x)

Figure 2.9

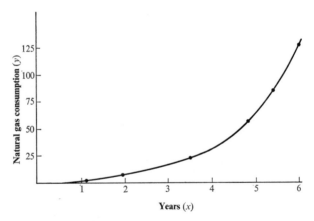

Years (x)

Figure 2.10

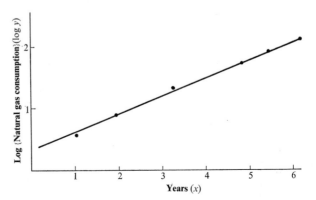

Years (x)

Contents

Acknowledgements

The five years the author spent as a special research fellow with the Building Services Research Unit (then the Hospital Engineering Research Unit) at the University of Glasgow are his main qualification for writing this book.

In December 1959, the Nuffield Provincial Hospitals Trust set up the Hospital Engineering Research Unit to investigate problems relating to the planning, installation and maintenance of engineering services in hospitals. Since that time, under inspired leadership, initially of Mr Harry Howard and currently of Mr William Carson, the Unit has made an intensive assault on the ramparts of ignorance and rule-of-thumb which exist round the problem of engineering service design. Many of the sections in this text draw directly on the work of the members of the BSRU; I trust they will accept, in good faith, this single and sincere acknowledgement of their efforts.

A list of the papers and reports produced by the BSRU can be obtained by writing to the University of Glasgow; I can think of no more lucrative source of information, and perhaps inspiration, for the student committed to the rational design of engineering services.

My thanks are due to Dr D. Fitzgerald, Head of the Science Division, the Heating and Ventilating Research Association, Mr Sean Mulcahy, of Varming Mulcahy Reilly Associates, and Professor T. A. Markus, Head of the Department of Architecture and Building Science, University of Strathclyde, for comment and correction which proved invaluable at the drafting stage of the text. Mr Peter Reed, my colleague at the Strathclyde School of Architecture, used the draft text for the re-structuring and implementation of the building services course for undergraduates and I am indebted to him for the valuable feedback which this exercise provided.

Tom Maver
University of Strathclyde, Glasgow
April 1970

1 Introduction

Architecture is more and more being recognized as the application of special skills to the problem of the design of complex environmental systems. The concept of the building as a complex system is not new, but little work has been done to develop it to a stage where the systematic techniques applicable in other fields of design endeavour are paralleled in architecture. The first task of this book, therefore, is to propose a design schema in which the engineering services are seen as an integral sub-system within the building system as a whole, in an effort to identify the design objectives and develop the methodologies for realizing them.

A design schema

It is safe to say, in the western world at least, that no social, commercial or industrial organization can properly fulfil its function without a dependence on the built environment; education needs schools, health needs hospitals, commerce needs offices, industry needs factories, families need homes. The difficulty for the building designer, however, is that the needs are often complex and conflicting, indeterminate and transient. None the less, the starting point is a statement of the objectives of the client organization; in Figure 1.1 the

Figure 1.1

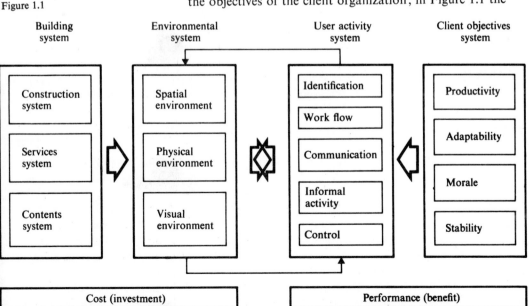

Building system	Environmental system	User activity system	Client objectives system
Construction system	Spatial environment	Identification	Productivity
		Work flow	
Services system	Physical environment	Communication	Adaptability
		Informal activity	Morale
Contents system	Visual environment	Control	Stability

Cost (investment)	Performance (benefit)

right-hand column represents a 'client objectives system' expressed in general terms. Arising from a statement of objectives is an expression of the 'user activities system' necessary to implement these objectives. At the other end of the diagram the 'building system' is seen as giving rise to the 'environmental system' and the crux of the design problem is the interface between the environmental system and the activities system. The interaction between the environmental system and the activities system is represented by two arrows to indicate that the environmental system may modify (promote *or* inhibit) the activities, and that the activities effect a change in the environment. In any building there exists a state of dynamic balance at this environment/ activities interface.

As a whole, the model illustrated in Figure 1.1 (which was developed by the Building Performance Research Unit and first set down by Markus[1]) represents a systematic view of the building design problem in general terms. It is not too difficult in the specific case of a local education authority, a regional hospital board or even a speculative office developer to replace the general sub-systems which make up the objectives and activities systems with those appropriate to the particular situation.

The formulation of a design objective function is possible, using the model in Figure 1.1. Associated with the building system there is a 'cost of provision'; associated with the environmental system is a 'running cost', i.e., a cost of providing and maintaining the environment over the life of the building. Together these 'costs-in-use' (see Chapter 4) represent the client's investment in the building. On the other side of the interface measures can be made of the degree to which activities can be successfully carried out and to which objectives are realized; together these 'performance' measures represent the benefit which the building gives to the client. Thus an optimum design can be defined as *that which maximizes the return on the client's investment.*

It should be noted that such an explicit formulation of the design objective function in no way precludes consideration of the psychological, sociological or aesthetic variables, provided the requirements are explicitly stated in the objectives or activities system and that a measure is available for the degree to which they are met. In the best of all possible worlds, of course, the investment and the benefit could be measured on identical scales – probably cost – and the optimization procedure would be simple; in the real world, however, the scales on which each of the performance measures are made may be different, necessitating a subjective weighting between them.

A further use to which the model can be put is that of helping to identify the interactions between individual sub-systems. Figure 1.2 shows the building system and the environmental system and the primary interactions between the services sub-system and the other sub-systems.

Services system/construction system
As will be shown in later sections of this text, the interaction between the construction system and the services system is considerable. The choice of materials and the area of fenestration have implications for the thermal response of the building and hence for the supply and distribution of services. The ease with which pipes and cables can be distributed throughout the building will of course be affected by the general configuration of the structural members and the detailed design of beams, slabs, etc.

Services system/contents system
If contents are defined to include the engineering services

Figure 1.2

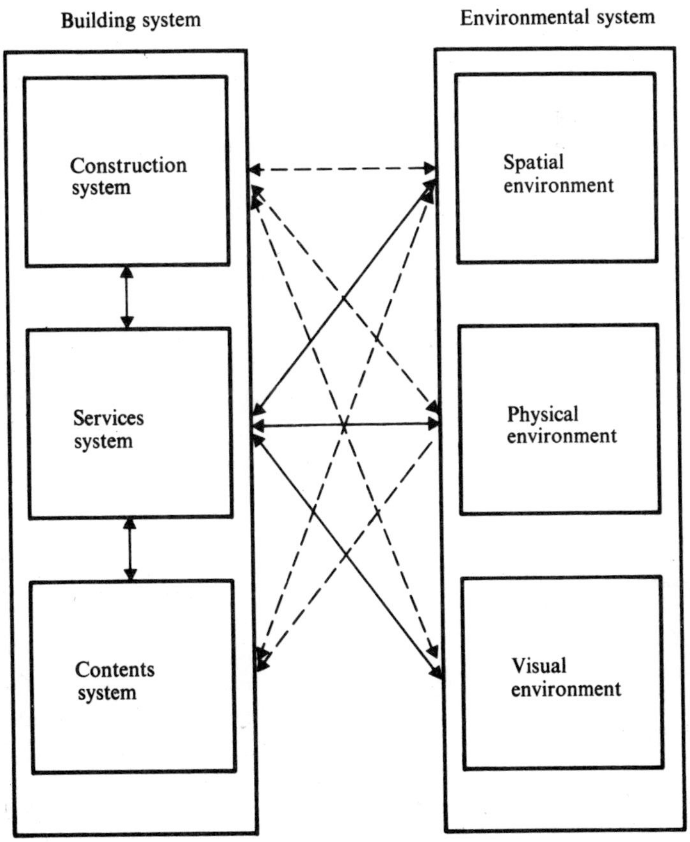

Building system   Environmental system

9

outlets – e.g., light fittings, electrical sockets, sanitary fixtures, heaters, etc. – then the interaction between these two systems is obvious. Other elements of the contents system – furniture, floor, wall and ceiling finishes – by affecting the lighting, acoustic and thermal properties of the building also interact with the services system.

Services system/physical environment
The main function of the services system is to create and maintain a desired level of physical environment and it is primarily with this interaction that the book deals.

Services system/spatial environment
The spatial layout of the building and the supply and distribution of services interact because of the fact that the positioning of demand points, relative to the supply point, influences the magnitude and configuration of pipe and cable runs. The orientation of the building and the relative location of sources of heat gain and heat loss will have a direct effect on the supply and distribution of the heating and cooling systems.

Services system/visual environment
The degree to which services plant and distribution runs are expressed visually will obviously affect the internal and external visual environment.

The growing importance of engineering services

One of the most marked trends in architecture over the centuries has been that of replacing the functions of the building structure by engineering service systems. In earliest times the mass of the structure provided security and protection from climatic extremes, and openings in the structure provided light and ventilation. Over the years the function of security has been partly taken over by electronic control devices and the function of moderating climatic variation has been taken over by heating and cooling plant; some of the functions of the window, the provision of light and ventilation, are now performed by engineering systems.

It is a matter of some debate as to whether or not this trend is a good one; it may be that it is more economic to allow the structure to perform these 'portmanteau' functions. The trend is not likely to be reversed, however, because the increased control which individual services afford over the built environment is now the norm expected by users of all building types. All the evidence points to pressure for greater control in the future.

A biological analogy may be instructive. The distributive networks of the engineering services can be likened to the veins, arteries and nerves of a living creature, transporting matter and energy throughout the structure. Building design has tended to parallel nature's move away from massive and exoskeletal structures with rudimentary distributive systems to light structures with complex distributive systems.

It has already been shown that the services system interacts with a large number of other sub-systems. To obtain a measure of its relative importance, the capital cost investment in services can be obtained for different building types and shown in context, as in Figure 1.3. Of the gross national product in the UK, 16% relates to capital items, i.e., cars, bridges, aeroplanes, ships, roads and other physical artifacts.

Of the 16%, the products of the building industry amount to almost half – 43%. This 43% may be apportioned in a number of different ways; in Figure 1.3, the division is made between industrialized building of all types (33%) and non-industrialized building of housing (17%), other building in the private sector (27%) and other building in the public sector (22%). Three specific examples of housing (a self-contained house), public building (a hospital) and private building (a factory) have been taken to show the apportionment between elements of the building – substructure, superstructure, services, finishes and fittings. The importance of the services is quite different in each of these three building types – 12% in the house, 18% in the factory and 50% in the hospital.

A breakdown of the capital investment in hospital engineering services has been attempted and shows an apportionment of 32% to electrical services, 27% to central plant (boilers, etc.) and main distribution (steam, etc.), 20% to the heating and ventilating services, 14% to hot and cold water services and 7% to gas and other services. This breakdown has been chosen from a host of alternative methods of apportioning capital cost for two reasons – it reflects the elemental divisions currently adopted in cost analyses, and it relates to the structure of the subject matter in Chapters 5 and 6 in this book.

As will be forcefully stated in Chapter 4, consideration of investment in capital cost terms alone is less than wise. Unfortunately, reliable statistics on the running costs of the various elements of buildings are not readily available; what data there are however, indicate that the percentage of total running costs of building types attributable to the

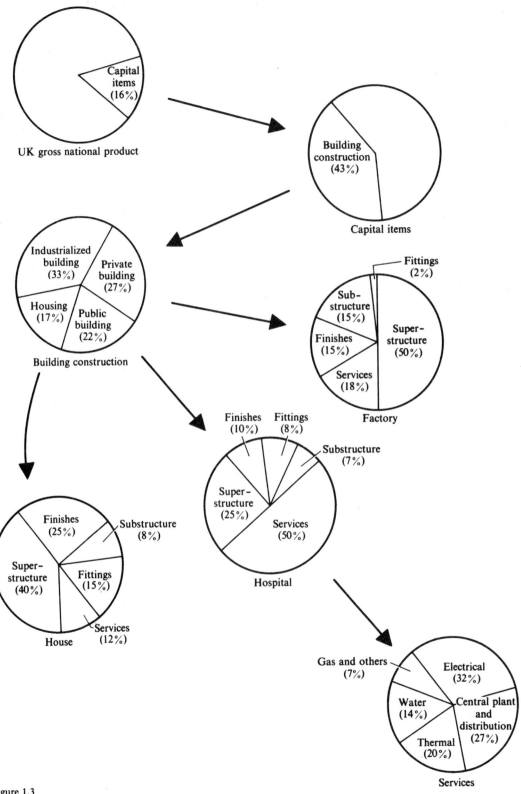

Figure 1.3

engineering services is proportionately greater than the percentage of total capital costs. Thus the true investment in services in, say, a hospital may be more than the investment of all the other elements combined – sub-structure, superstructure, fittings and finishes.

The nature of the services design problem

The basic problem in engineering services design is one of supply and demand, of satisfying increasingly exacting needs in the face of nature's increasing entropy. As with the world food supply and demand, the problem is less one of limited resources at a global level than one of the mis-match between resources and needs with respect to time and space. Accelerating advances in technology increase the possibility of overcoming the spatial and temporal mis-match, but mankind has yet to become competent in measuring the intensity of different needs, the interaction between them, and the level of investment which should be made to satisfy them in order to ensure a maximum return. In short, we possess an understanding of the technical elements of the system but lack an understanding of the operating characteristics of the system as a whole.

Technological boldness has led to the creation of systems which are at present in operation and which affect everyday life but of which no one has any true operational understanding. A sub-set of these systems (although perhaps minor when compared to, say, transport systems or the international monetary system) are the engineering services in buildings. Money is invested to generate heat and more money is invested to remove heat; money is invested to convert heat to electricity and more money is invested to convert electricity back to heat; money is invested in plant with a working life of 40 years, capable of meeting demands which will occur only once in 5000 years, whereas investment in other plant is insufficient to meet a daily recurring demand.

All of this is surprising enough, but when it is considered that this state of affairs is current at a time when man is able to journey to the moon, explore its surface and return safely to earth, the ludicrous aspect of endeavour in the field of building design is all too apparent. One reason for the success of the lunar programme was of course the magnitude of the investment made in it. There are, however, other reasons:

(a) unlike the services systems in buildings (which have grown like Topsy) the systems which were relevant to the moon shot were conceived and designed from a virtually *tabula rasa* situation,

(b) to this *tabula rasa* situation were applied the most up-to-date operational techniques for the study of complex systems, including statistical decision theory, operational research and large-scale computer simulation,

(c) a significant proportion of the total budget was invested in *a priori* research and in the monitoring of the performance characteristics of earlier preparatory orbital flights, and

(d) demarcation between professional disciplines was forgotten in the pursuit of a common, clearly expressed, goal.

There are many who would argue that the pay-off from the lunar programme was insufficient to justify the large investment made. Be that as it may, a way of increasing the pay-off is to apply the decision-making methodologies, so convincingly demonstrated during the programme, to the design of other less dramatic but perhaps more important complex systems – including the services systems in buildings.

The main considerations in the study of engineering service systems in buildings are threefold:
(a) the statistical laws by which the probabilistic nature of demand for the services may be ordered and understood,
(b) the laws of natural philosophy which govern the conversion and distribution of energy and matter, and
(c) the economic laws which provide a basis for comparison between alternative solutions.

Chapters 2, 3 and 4 of this book are an attempt to set down some of these laws in so far as they relate to engineering service design; it will be realized, however, that in a volume such as this it is possible only to outline the theory, and the strongest recommendations are made that the serious student studies the works listed at the end of the book.

Chapter 5 deals with individual sub-systems, covering:
(a) hot and cold water services,
(b) electrical services,
(c) gas services,
(d) heating and air conditioning,
and Chapter 6 attempts a synthesis of these sub-systems into a rational whole.

Obviously a number of engineering service systems has been excluded – drainage, control and information systems, and mechanical handling systems. Those which are included represent the main cost investment in a typical building and exhibit a high degree of interdependence between each other and with the building as a whole; they therefore provide the best vehicle for development of the arguments put forward in this book. For those systems which are included, much more detailed text-books specific to each system, are available, and some are listed on pages 161–2.

The reader should bear in mind that this is a text on methodology, not on technology. It deals neither with the practical matters of regulations, bye-laws or codes, nor with the scientific study of physiological, sociological or psychological needs, but with the area of strategic decision-making which lies between. It is neither a handbook nor a learned treatise, but an introduction to systematic design thinking applied to engineering systems. Since the argument is developed progressively, it should be read right through from cover to cover.

2 The statistical laws of demand

The demand made on any system designed to satisfy human requirements will be variable because the behaviour of the human being, and of the natural environment in which he exists, are themselves variable; the climate varies from hour to hour and from day to day as do the desires and needs of the individual. Fortunately, although variable, demand is not wholly unpredictable and this chapter deals with the techniques available to the designer for the quantification and interpretation of demand data.

The notion of probability

For better, or worse, we live in a world in which the future is uncertain; the likelihood of certain events occurring is very high, e.g., the sun rising tomorrow morning or the incidence of a car accident somewhere in the UK within the next 24 hours, whereas the likelihood of other events, e.g., someone swimming the Atlantic Ocean, even in the next decade, is very low. Statisticians have defined a measure of relative likelihood, which they call **probability**, as follows: the probability of an event occurring is given by the ratio of the number of observed occurrences of the event to the total number of possible outcomes of the experiment.

The definition works quite well if one thinks, as statisticians mostly do, of an experiment in which a die is rolled 60 times. If the single spot turns up 10 times, the probability of the single spot occurring would be given by

$$\tfrac{10}{60} = \tfrac{1}{6} = 0.166\,\dot{6},$$

i.e., the ratio of the number of occurrences of the single spot to the total number of rolls of the die.

When one comes to consider engineering services, however, the interpretation of probability requires a little thought. Assume that in a 60-minute period a water tap is in use on five occasions, each use lasting two minutes. In terms of the definition there are 60 possible outcomes, equivalent to the 60 minutes of the study period; the number of these outcomes in which the event (i.e., usage of the tap) occurred is $5 \times 2 = 10$. Thus the probability is given by $\tfrac{10}{60} = 0.166\,\dot{6}$, as before. Since it is rather odd to think of units of time as the 'outcomes' of experiments, the definition of probability can be reformulated more in keeping with requirements, thus: the probability of a demand occurring is given by the ratio of the duration of the demand to the total study period.

In whatever form the definition is worded, the measure of probability must lie between zero and unity, with unity representing complete certainty.

Laws of probability

Armed with a definition which allows a numerical measure to be put on the concept, it is now possible to do some arithmetical manipulation. Take a pipe which supplies two taps A and B; the probability of A being in use, P_A, we shall assume to be $\frac{1}{5}$, and of B being in use P_B, $\frac{1}{2}$. The laws of probability (the validity of which can be checked by example) allow two statements to be made: the probability of A being in use **or** of B being in use is given by

$$(P_A + P_B) = \tfrac{1}{5} + \tfrac{1}{2} = \tfrac{7}{10}.$$

The probability of A being in use **and** of B being in use (simultaneously) is given by

$$(P_A \times P_B) = \tfrac{1}{5} \times \tfrac{1}{2} = \tfrac{1}{10}.$$

These statements are expressions, respectively, of the Additive Law and the Multiplicative Law of Probability and it is worth paying them heed since they are at the very heart of the design philosophy being proposed.

To illustrate further the Multiplicative Law, imagine a building with 10 electrical socket outlets, each of which has a probability of use of $p = 0.3$. The probability of all 10 being in simultaneous use is given by $(p)^n = (0.3)^{10} = 0.000\,000\,072\,9$. The probability of less than 10 being in simultaneous use is a little more complicated but can be computed from the formula:

probability of r out of n in use $= {}_nC_r(p)^r(1-p)^{n-r}$

$$\text{where } {}_nC_r = \frac{n!}{r!(n-r)!} \text{ and } n! \text{ is given}$$

by $(n)(n-1)(n-2) \ldots (1)$.

Table 2.1

Use of this formula gives rise to the following results:

Number in use	Formula	Probability	Accumulative total
0	$(0\cdot7)^{10}$	$p_0 = 0\cdot028$	0·028
1	$_{10}C_1(0\cdot3)^1(0\cdot7)^9$	$p_1 = 0\cdot121$	0·149
2	$_{10}C_2(0\cdot3)^2(0\cdot7)^8$	$p_2 = 0\cdot233$	0·382
3	$_{10}C_3(0\cdot3)^3(0\cdot7)^7$	$p_3 = 0\cdot266$	0·649
4	$_{10}C_4(0\cdot3)^4(0\cdot7)^6$	$p_4 = 0\cdot200$	0·849
5	$_{10}C_5(0\cdot3)^5(0\cdot7)^5$	$p_5 = 0\cdot102$	0·952
6	$_{10}C_6(0\cdot3)^6(0\cdot7)^4$	$p_6 = 0\cdot036$	0·989
7	$_{10}C_7(0\cdot3)^7(0\cdot7)^3$	$p_7 = 0\cdot001$	0·990
8	$_{10}C_8(0\cdot3)^8(0\cdot7)^2$	$p_8 = 0\cdot000$	0·990
9	$_{10}C_9(0\cdot3)^9(0\cdot7)^1$	$p_9 = 0\cdot000$	0·990
10	$(0\cdot3)^{10}$	$p_{10} = 0\cdot000$	0·990

The implication these results have for the designer is very important: by reference to the accumulative total he can design for five outlets in use simultaneously and have a 95% probability of satisfying the entire demand, or he can design for seven outlets and have a 99% probability of satisfying the entire demand. In any event, such a computation will give him cause to hesitate to design for 10 in use simultaneously since such an eventuality has a probability of occurrence of only 0·000 000 072 9.

Frequency distribution of demand

Having established the basic laws of probability, it is appropriate now to employ them as a means of making a clear statement as to the demand in any situation.

Binomial frequency distribution
Taking the 10 electrical socket outlets as before, a 'probability density function' can be constructed, as in Figure 2.1. This

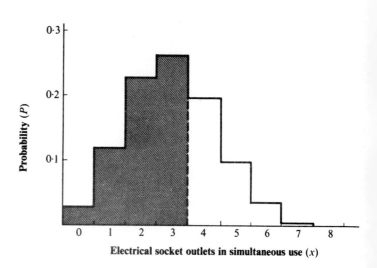

Figure 2.1

Electrical socket outlets in simultaneous use (x)

figure is such that the area under the graph is equal to unity, and the area under that part of it from zero outlets up to x outlets (evaluated in the 'Accumulative Total' column in Table 2.1) gives the probability of x or fewer outlets being in simultaneous use. As drawn, the shaded area represents the probability of three outlets or less in simultaneous use, the unshaded area represents four outlets or more in simultaneous use. Had 1000 observations been made of the building in which these outlets are situated, the frequencies of observing 1, 2, 3, 4, etc., could be expected to be $1000p_1$, $1000p_2$, $1000p_3$, etc., and from the observations the 'frequency distribution' of demand could have been constructed, as shown in Figure 2.2.

The value of a frequency distribution is that it gives a clear picture of what the character of the demand is like. In this case the most frequently occurring event is three outlets in use simultaneously, and the frequency of more than three in use tapers off progressively. It is possible, however, to be even more explicit: two measures can be used to uniquely describe this distribution – the mean, a measure of central tendency of the distribution, and the standard deviation, a measure of the spread of the distribution.

The mean, $\bar{x}$, is defined by

$$\bar{x} = \frac{\Sigma f x}{\Sigma f}$$

and the standard deviation, s, is defined by

$$s = \sqrt{\left(\frac{\Sigma f x^2}{\Sigma f} - (\bar{x})^2\right)}.$$

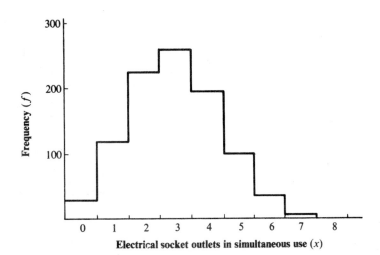

Figure 2.2

Electrical socket outlets in simultaneous use (x)

Some care must be exercised by those unfamiliar with statistical notation and it is perhaps worthwhile to go through the computation of these two measures in detail to obviate any algebraic misunderstandings.

Table 2.2

f	x	fx	fx^2
28	0	0	0
121	1	121	121
233	2	466	932
267	3	801	2403
200	4	800	3200
103	5	515	2565
38	6	228	1368
1	7	7	49
0	8	0	0
0	9	0	0
0	10	0	0
1000		2938	10 638

thus $\bar{x} = \dfrac{\Sigma fx}{\Sigma f} = \dfrac{2938}{1000} = 2\cdot938,$

and $s = \sqrt{\left(\dfrac{\Sigma fx^2}{\Sigma f} - (\bar{x})^2\right)} = \sqrt{\left(\dfrac{10\ 638}{1000} - (2\cdot938)^2\right)} = 1\cdot55.$

The formulae quoted can be applied to any frequency distribution to obtain the mean and the standard deviation. The case which has just been considered, however, is a rather special one: the variable under examination, x (the number of outlets in use simultaneously) varies discretely, i.e., increases by one whole unit at a time; the minimum number in use is zero; and the maximum possible number in use is finite (in this case 10). These characteristics classify the distribution as being **binomial** and allow a simplification of the general formulae to be stated, as follows:

$$\bar{x} = np \tag{1}$$
$$s = \sqrt{(npq)} \tag{2}$$

where n = maximum possible value of the variable (i.e., maximum possible number of outlets in use simultaneously),

p = probability of any event occurring (i.e., the probability of any one outlet being in use),

and $q = (1-p)$ (i.e., the probability of any one outlet not being in use).

Thus, from (1)

$$2 \cdot 938 = np$$
i.e., $2 \cdot 938 = 10p$
i.e., $p = 0 \cdot 293\ 8 \fallingdotseq 0 \cdot 3$, as would be expected.

The foregoing provides the designer with two approaches to the assessment of demand which is binomial in character:

(a) he can determine by observation the basic probability of a single event occurring, p, and build up the frequency distribution by computation, or

(b) he can observe the frequency distribution of simultaneous usage and from this compute n and p.

In either case he has a full description of the demand and an unambiguous measure of it, namely, a binomial demand with a mean of $2 \cdot 938$ and a standard deviation of $1 \cdot 55$.

Normal frequency distribution

What has been discussed under the subheading 'Binomial frequency distribution' applies in the simple case of discrete uses or non-uses of a particular facility – electrical outlets, taps, etc., but in many cases the designer is interested in measures of the quantity of energy or of a utility demanded within a set period of time. To cope with this situation, where the variable is continuous in nature, i.e., can be of any numerical value, the **normal** frequency distribution is most useful.

Assume that the following table of data gives the number of cubic metres of town gas consumed in a canteen kitchen each day for 40 consecutive days:

Table 2.3

32	36	41	38
39	40	42	33
28	31	36	43
47	45	53	27
36	47	44	48
37	50	29	36
51	38	30	44
43	34	46	34
33	35	23	52
42	58	37	46

The method of constructing the frequency distribution is to plot the frequency with which observations fall within ranges of the variable under investigation. The choice of ranges of the variable is arbitrary and in this case will be set as shown:

Table 2.4

Gas consumption in cubic metres per day	Frequency of observation
19·5–24·5	1
24·5–29·5	3
29·5–34·5	7
34·5–39·5	10
39·5–44·5	8
44·5–49·5	6
49·5–54·5	4
54·5–59·5	1

When the frequencies have been established, the frequency distribution can be plotted using the midpoint of the ranges of the variable as a horizontal scale (Figure 2.3). The nature of the demand now has a visual representation and can be seen to be 'bell-shaped' – the classical configuration of the normal frequency distribution. It remains, as before, to compute the mean and standard deviation according to the general formulae, thus:

$$\text{mean, } \bar{x} = \frac{\Sigma fx}{\Sigma f} = 39\cdot5$$

$$\text{standard deviation, } s = \sqrt{\left(\frac{\Sigma fx^2}{\Sigma f} - (\bar{x})^2\right)} = 6\cdot2.$$

With the binomial distribution, it was possible to compute the area under any part of the distribution to obtain the probability of the demand being equal to or less than a given

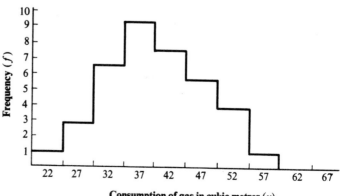

Figure 2.3

Consumption of gas in cubic metres (x)

22

amount. This is also possible with the normal distribution but as the algebra is a little complicated, it is easier to employ statistical tables. To calculate the demand for a given probability, the equation:

demand $= \bar{x} + vs$

where v is given by the following table, may be used.

Table 2.5

Probability	v
0·5	0
0·6	0·253
0·7	0·524
0·8	0·842
0·9	1·281
0·95	1·645
0·99	2·326
0·999	3·090

The designer is now in a position to say that if he desires to accept a probability of 0·95 of satisfying the demand for town gas, he must arrange to make available

$\{39·5 + (1·645 \times 6·2)\} = 49·7$ cubic metres per day.

Put another, less statistically exact, way, he can claim that in providing 50 cubic metres per day he is satisfying 95% of the demand.

In theory, a variable conforms to a normal frequency distribution only if it is continuous and has an infinite upper and lower limit. The consumption of town gas is certainly continuous but the lower limit is obviously zero and the upper limit is constrained by the size of the supply system; for practical purposes, however, the upper and lower limits are sufficiently far from the mean as to be effectively infinite.

Before leaving the theory of the normal distribution, a further point must be developed. Assume that the mean, $\bar{x}$, and standard deviation, s, apply to one of an identical set of N frequency distributions. Then the mean of the entire set is given by $N\bar{x}$ and the standard deviation of the entire set is given by $\sqrt{(N)}vs$. This means that if two canteen kitchens on the same site are to be supplied with town gas, the demand, for 0·95 probability, is given by:

demand $= N\bar{x} + \sqrt{(N)}vs$
$\quad\quad\quad = 2(39·5) + \sqrt{(2)} \times 1·645 \times 6·2$
$\quad\quad\quad = 93·4.$

Obviously 93·4 cubic metres per day is less than two times 49·7 cubic metres per day; the reason for this is that the maximum demand in both kitchens is unlikely to occur on the same day. This is an example of the concept of *diversity* of demand, which is of paramount importance in efficient engineering service design. Figure 2.4 illustrates the advantage to be gained in supplying up to 20 similar buildings or parts of buildings from a single source as opposed to meeting the demand in each separately; the mean and the standard deviation for one element are taken as 20 and 10 respectively. While there is no simple statistical expression for the diversity of demand in *dissimilar* buildings or parts of buildings, it will be clear that there will be a tendency towards greater diversity between dissimilar units than between similar units due to the fact that activities, and hence needs, will be more diverse.

Other frequency distributions
Two other frequency distributions are worth mentioning: the **Poisson** distribution applicable to discrete events where the probability of an individual event occurring is low and the upper limit to the number of simultaneously occurring events is very high, and the **negative exponential** distribution applicable to a continuous variable with zero minimum and infinite maximum. A summary of the equations, characteristics and applications of all four distributions is contained in Table 2.6.

Regression and correlation

So far, the theory which has been covered is applicable to the investigation of individual variables, e.g., consumption of water, air temperature, usage of electrical outlets. The ability of the designer to predict demand is greatly enhanced, however, if he can establish a correlation between demand

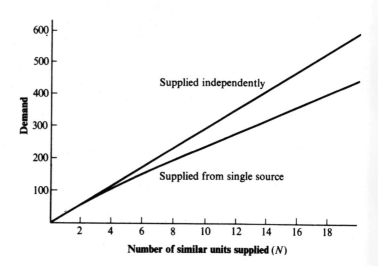

Figure 2.4

	Mean ($\bar{x}$)	Standard deviation(s)	Equation	Characteristics	Applications
Normal	$\dfrac{\Sigma fx}{\Sigma f}$	$\sqrt{\dfrac{\Sigma fx^2}{\Sigma f} - (\bar{x})^2}$	$P(r_1 \leqslant r \leqslant r_2)$ $= \dfrac{1}{\sqrt{(2\pi)}s} \int_{r_1}^{r_2} e^{-\frac{(x-\bar{x})^2}{2s^2}}$	symmetrical continuous min $= -\infty$ max $= +\infty$	daily, hourly, weekly, monthly, annual consumption of water, gas, electricity, medical gases, conditioned air, etc.; costs; climatic conditions—air temperature, rainfall, etc.
Binomial	$\dfrac{\Sigma fx}{\Sigma f}$ $= np$	$\sqrt{\dfrac{\Sigma fx^2}{\Sigma f} - (\bar{x})^2}$ $= \sqrt{npq}$	$P(r) = {}_nC_r p^r (1-p)^{n-r}$	skew discrete min $= 0$ max $= n$	usage of taps, electrical socket outlets, telephones, w.c.'s, medical gas outlets, bunsen burners, incinerators, etc.; defects in components produced in batches
Poisson	$\dfrac{\Sigma fx}{\Sigma f}$ $= \lambda$	$\sqrt{\dfrac{\Sigma fx^2}{\Sigma f} - (\bar{x})^2}$ $= \sqrt{\lambda}$	$P(r) = \dfrac{e^{-\lambda}\lambda^r}{r!}$	skew discrete min $= 0$ max $= +\infty$	as above, when p$\rightarrow$0 and n$\rightarrow\infty$; incidence of accident; maintenance needs; breakdowns
Negative exponential	$\dfrac{\Sigma fx}{\Sigma f}$ $= \dfrac{1}{\lambda}$	$\sqrt{\dfrac{\Sigma fx^2}{\Sigma f} - (\bar{x})^2}$ $= \dfrac{1}{\lambda}$	$P(r_1 \leqslant r \leqslant r_2)$ $= \int_{r_1}^{r_2} \lambda e^{-\lambda r} dr$	skew continuous min $= 0$ max $= +\infty$	interval between events which are themselves described by Poisson, e.g., time between usage of outlets, taps, lifts, incinerators; physical distance between electrical cable faults, etc.; time between breakdown, maintenance needs, etc.

Table 2.6

and a known variable; if, for instance, he can relate oxygen consumption in a hospital ward unit to the number of beds, he is able, at an early stage in design when the ward size is known, to compute from the relationship the likely oxygen consumption.

Consider two variables, x and y, which from observation are related, as shown in Figure 2.5. There is some justification for assuming that they are linearly related, but clearly the observations are somewhat scattered on either side of any straight line drawn through them. If the level of the dependent variable, y, is to be computed for any given level of the independent variable x, then there is a need to construct a line through the data which will minimize the y-distance of all the observations from the line.

Taking the general equation of such a line to be

$$y = ax + b,$$

where a is the slope of the line and b is the distance from the origin to the intercept on the y axis, the task is to evaluate a and b. Fortunately, statisticians have developed the appropriate equations and these can be quoted as:

$$a = \frac{N\Sigma xy - \Sigma x \Sigma y}{N\Sigma x^2 - (\Sigma x)^2}$$

$$b = \frac{\Sigma x^2 \Sigma y - \Sigma x \Sigma xy}{N\Sigma x^2 - (\Sigma x)^2}$$

where N = the number of pairs of observations.

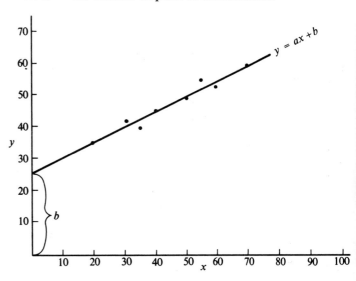

Figure 2.5

26

Again, the statistical symbols can lead to confusion for the uninitiated and it is worthwhile working through the computation as follows:

Table 2.7

x	y	xy	x^2	y^2
20	35	700	400	1225
30	42	1260	900	1764
35	40	1400	1225	1600
40	46	1840	1600	2116
50	49	2450	2500	2401
55	55	3025	3025	3025
60	53	3180	3600	2809
70	60	4200	4900	3600
360	380	18055	18150	18540

Thus,

$$a = \frac{8(18\,055) - (360 \times 380)}{8(18\,150) - (360 \times 360)} = 0 \cdot 49$$

and $$b = \frac{18\,150(380) - 360(18\,055)}{8(18\,150) - (360 \times 360)} = 25 \cdot 45.$$

The equation of the straight line can now be quoted as

$$y = 0 \cdot 49x + 25 \cdot 45$$

and is known as the 'linear regression of y on x'.

If x and y were in fact observations respectively of glazed area (in square metres) and heating cost (in pounds sterling) gathered from existing buildings, the designer now has a tool with which to compute heating costs in a new design. If he proposes to have 45 square metres of glass, an estimate of the heating cost is given by:

heating cost, $y = 0 \cdot 49(45) + 25 \cdot 45 = $ **47·5**.

A warning must be sounded about being overly daring in extrapolating from a linear regression equation; while the assumption of linearity may be justified over the range of observations available, there is no evidence that the relationship is linear beyond the observed range.

A measure of correlation between the two variables can be computed as follows:

$$\text{correlation coefficient, } r = \frac{\Sigma xy - N\bar{x}\bar{y}}{\sqrt{\{\Sigma x^2 - N(\bar{x})^2\}}\sqrt{\{\Sigma y^2 - N(\bar{y})^2\}}}$$

and in the example under consideration the result

$$r = 0\cdot97$$

is obtained. By definition, the value of r lies between -1 and $+1$. When r is close to -1 in value, there is said to be 'high negative correlation' and the regression line slopes downwards from left to right; when r is close to $+1$, there is said to be 'high positive correlation' and the regression line slopes upwards from left to right; when r is close to zero there is no significant correlation between the two variables.

Multiple regression
The method of dealing with two variables which are linearly related has been described; this method can be extended, at the price of simplicity, to describe the relationship between the dependent variable, y, and a number of independent variables, x_1, x_2, x_3, etc. The appropriate computational steps can be found in statistical text-books and will not be covered here, but the reader may be interested in an example of the use of this technique in the prediction of the average daily hot water consumption in hospital paediatric ward units. The multiple linear regression gave the relationship:
average daily consumption $= 25 + 22x_1 + 1\cdot6x_2$
where $x_1 =$ number of beds in the ward, and
$x_2 =$ a measure of the level of water outlet provision.

Variations with time and season
The value of the techniques already described is of course dependent on the validity of the basic observations which have had to be made in existing buildings; it would be ludicrous to do analyses on the demand for electricity if the basic data had been gathered only during the daylight hours. It is important, therefore, to scrutinize basic observation of demand for variations with time and season.

Figure 2.6 gives the quarterly consumption of electricity (in GJ) over six years in a hospital. There is clearly a trend towards increased consumption, but the picture is somewhat obscured by the dramatic seasonal fluctuation in demand. Since any new building to be designed may have a life of up to 60 years, it is important that future trends be fully taken account of. Similarly, if a detailed, short-term study is to be made of hour-by-hour consumption it is necessary to make allowance for the seasonal variation.

The method of establishing the basic trend is to compute the regression equation with the independent variable x, representing time units, and the dependent variable y, representing consumption. In the example given, x is taken as the number of quarters, from 1 to 24 and y as the GJ consumption; the regression equation is calculated to be

$$y = 9 \cdot 640x + 554 \cdot 333$$

and the relationship can be used as a basis for the computa-

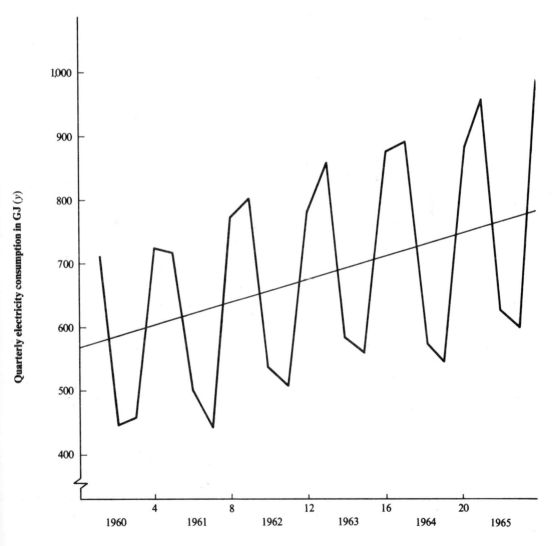

Figure 2.6

Quarterly periods (x)

tion of future growth in demand, subject to the provision on pages 30–1.

Measures of seasonal variation can now be calculated by taking-off the distance between both peaks and troughs and the computed trend line. In this example there is a seasonal variation of ± 166 GJ.

Growth of demand over time for engineering services conforms less often to a straight line than to an exponential curve which has the form

$$y = ba^x.$$

Taking logarithms of both sides gives

$$\log y = x \log a + \log b$$

which is the general form of the equation of a straight line with

$\log y$ substituted for y
$\log a$ substituted for a, and
$\log b$ substituted for b.

With these substitutions made, the values of $\log a$ and $\log b$, and hence of a and b, are obtained according to the equations given earlier.

Forecasting and prediction; a cautionary note
Throughout this chapter techniques have been described which facilitate the estimation of demand in new buildings; they don't, however, provide the designer with an infallible crystal ball. No amount of algebraic manipulation can determine the future.

A host of dangers accompanies statistical analysis: the sample of data drawn from existing buildings must be sufficiently large and without bias as to time of day, week, season and year, geographical location, observational technique etc., etc.; the appropriate theoretical distribution – normal, binomial, Poisson, negative exponential – must be presumed; the significance of conclusions must be checked using more advanced techniques which it has not been possible to discuss here. It is therefore advisable before trying anything too bold to engage the services of a statistician or to make a proper and thorough study of the subject.

None the less, the techniques covered in this chapter should facilitate the estimation of demand for engineering services in a new building. It is worthwhile supplementing the techniques of forecast – i.e., of casting past data forward – with an attempt at prediction – i.e., the divining of changing circumstances (particularly technological innovation) which will impinge on the usage of the engineering services.

Worked examples

Problem

(1) To determine the size of a water pipe supplying 10 outlets, it is assumed that the probability (p) that any one of them is in use at a given time is 0·15. If it can also be assumed that the usage of each outlet is independent of the use of others, calculate the mean and standard deviation of the distribution of the number of outlets in use at the same time. What is the probability that three outlets will be in use simultaneously? How many outlets must be considered in use simultaneously to satisfy 99% of the demand?

Answer

Since the variable (number of outlets in use simultaneously) is discrete with a finite limit of 0 and finite upper limit of 10, the binomial distribution will be assumed to be applicable. The probability of r outlets in use simultaneously is given as

$$P(r) = {}_nC_r p^r (1-p)^{n-r}.$$

Thus,

		Accumulative total
$P(0) = {}_{10}C_0\ (0{\cdot}15)^0\ (0{\cdot}85)^{10} = 0{\cdot}198\,674\,400$	$= 0{\cdot}198\,674\,400$
$P(1) = {}_{10}C_1\ (0{\cdot}15)^1\ (0{\cdot}85)^9\ = 0{\cdot}347\,425\,420$	$= 0{\cdot}544\,299\,820$
$P(2) = {}_{10}C_2\ (0{\cdot}15)^2\ (0{\cdot}85)^8\ = 0{\cdot}275\,896\,650$	$= 0{\cdot}820\,196\,470$
$P(3) = {}_{10}C_3\ (0{\cdot}15)^3\ (0{\cdot}85)^7\ = 0{\cdot}129\,833\,720$	$= 0{\cdot}950\,030\,190$
$P(4) = {}_{10}C_4\ (0{\cdot}15)^4\ (0{\cdot}85)^6\ = 0{\cdot}040\,095\,707$	$= 0{\cdot}990\,125\,900$
$P(5) = {}_{10}C_5\ (0{\cdot}15)^5\ (0{\cdot}85)^5\ = 0{\cdot}008\,490\,856$	$= 0{\cdot}998\,616\,750$
$P(6) = {}_{10}C_6\ (0{\cdot}15)^6\ (0{\cdot}85)^4\ = 0{\cdot}001\,248\,655$	$= 0{\cdot}999\,865\,410$
$P(7) = {}_{10}C_7\ (0{\cdot}15)^7\ (0{\cdot}85)^3\ = 0{\cdot}000\,016\,762$	$= 0{\cdot}999\,882\,170$
$P(8) = {}_{10}C_8\ (0{\cdot}15)^8\ (0{\cdot}85)^2\ = 0{\cdot}000\,001\,109$	$= 0{\cdot}999\,883\,280$
$P(9) = {}_{10}C_9\ (0{\cdot}15)^9\ (0{\cdot}85)^1\ = 0{\cdot}000\,000\,043$	$= 0{\cdot}999\,883\,320$
$P(10) = {}_{10}C_{10}(0{\cdot}15)^{10}(0{\cdot}85)^0\ = 0{\cdot}000\,000\,006$	$= 0{\cdot}999\,883\,330$

The probability of three outlets (no more, no less) being in use simultaneously is given by $P(3)$, i.e., **0·129 833 720**. (Note that the probability of *three or less* being in simultaneous use is given by the 'Accumulative total' column, and is equal to 0·950 030 190.)

To obtain the number in simultaneous use which must be provided for to satisfy 99% of the demand, the 'Accumulative total' column is scanned for that number which is just greater than 0·99. This turns out to be 0·990 125 900 which indicates that *four* outlets in simultaneous use have to be catered for. Figure 2.7 illustrates the shape of the probability density function.

In the text the formulae for mean and standard deviation were given as

$$\bar{x} = \frac{\Sigma fx}{\Sigma f}$$

$$s = \sqrt{\left(\frac{\Sigma fx^2}{\Sigma f} - (\bar{x})^2\right)}.$$

The numerical values of mean and standard deviation are unaltered by substituting for frequency of observation, f, the appropriate value of probability, thus:

$$\bar{x} = \frac{\Sigma Px}{\Sigma P}$$

$$s = \sqrt{\left(\frac{\Sigma Px^2}{\Sigma P} - (\bar{x})^2\right)}.$$

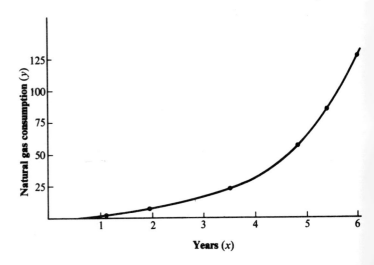

Figure 2.7

The data therefore read (abbreviating the probability values to three decimal places):

Number in use (x)	P	Px	Px²
0	0·197	0	0
1	0·374	0·374	0·374
2	0·256	0·512	1·024
3	0·130	0·390	1·170
4	0·040	0·160	0·640
5	0·008	0·040	0·200
6	0·001	0·006	0·036
7	0	0	0
8	0	0	0
9	0	0	0
10	0	0	0
	1	1·482	3·444

$$.\text{e., } \bar{x} = \frac{\Sigma Px}{\Sigma P} = \mathbf{1 \cdot 482}$$

$$s = \sqrt{\left(\frac{\Sigma Px^2}{\Sigma P} - (\bar{x})^2\right)} = \mathbf{1 \cdot 117}.$$

Alternatively, the mean and standard deviation can be computed from the relationships

$$\bar{x} = np$$
$$s = \sqrt{(npq)}$$
$$\text{i.e., } \bar{x} = 10 \times 0 \cdot 15 = \mathbf{1 \cdot 5}$$
$$s = \sqrt{(10 \times 0 \cdot 15 \times 0 \cdot 85)} = \mathbf{1 \cdot 125}.$$

Problem
(2) Readings from a meter which prints out the consumption in dm³ of hot water in a building every 24 hours are as follows:

362	436	485	590	463	340
390	532	459	423	503	417
498	525	371	455	406	417
481	465	397	506	520	
389	428	510	375	517	
495	456	437	402	405	
434	574	315	470	408	
469	473	462	451	427	
555	414	451	439	480	
392	467	467	473	547	

Construct the frequency distribution and compute the mean and standard deviation. Assuming a normal distribution, calculate the number of dm^3 per day which would be required to satisfy 95% of the demand. How many dm^3 per day are required to satisfy 95% of the demand in three identical buildings, supplied from a single source?

Answer
The first task is to decide on the ranges of the variable which will be used. The minimum and maximum readings are 315 and 590 respectively, i.e., the total range is 275. To obtain about 10 groups therefore, each group should have a range of, say, 30. The problem of a reading existing on the boundary between two groups is obviated if the boundaries are defined thus:
307·5–337·5
337·5–367·5
367·5–397·5
etc.

With the boundaries defined, the frequency with which readings fall into each range can be determined; this is best done by a system of 'tally-marks':

Range	Mid-point (x)	Tally-marks	Total
307·5-337·5	322·5	1	1
337·5-367·5	352·5	11	2
367·5-397·5	382·5	111111	6
397·5-427·5	412·5	111111111	9
427·5-457·5	442·5	1111111111	10
457·5-487·5	472·5	111111111111	12
487·5-517·5	502·5	111111	6
517·5-547·5	532·5	1111	4
547·5-577·5	562·5	11	2
577·5-607·5	592·5	1	1

Figure 2.8 illustrates the shape of the frequency distribution; from its shape and the fact that the variable is continuous, with very high and low limits, the assumption of normality seems quite reasonable.

Now, if the mean and standard deviation are to be calculated using the mid-points (x), some laborious arithmetic must be undertaken. Things can be simplified by subtracting, say, 442·5 from all values of x, and dividing by 30 to produce a new variable, say, X; the mean and standard deviation of this new variable, once calculated, can be adjusted to produce the mean and standard deviation of the original variable.

x	$X = \frac{x-442\cdot5}{30}$	f	fX	fX^2
322·5	−4	1	−4	16
352·5	−3	2	−6	18
382·5	−2	6	−12	24
412·5	−1	9	−9	9
442·5	0	10	0	0
472·5	+1	12	12	12
502·5	+2	6	12	24
532·5	+3	4	12	36
562·5	+4	2	8	32
592·5	+5	1	5	25
		53	18	196

$$\bar{X} = \frac{\Sigma fX}{\Sigma f} = \frac{18}{53} = 0\cdot34$$

$$s_X = \sqrt{\left(\frac{\Sigma fX^2}{\Sigma f} - (\bar{X})^2\right)} = \sqrt{\left(\frac{196}{53} - (0\cdot34)^2\right)} = 1\cdot89.$$

The means of the original and new variable are related exactly as the variables themselves, i.e.,

$$\bar{X} = \frac{\bar{x} - 442\cdot5}{30} \quad \text{i.e., } \bar{x} = \textbf{452·7}.$$

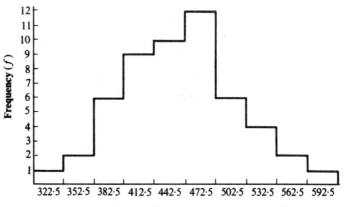

Consumption of hot water in cubic decimetres (x)

Figure 2.8

35

The standard deviations, being independent of the mean values, are related thus:

$$s_X = \frac{s_x}{30} \quad \text{i.e., } s_x = 1\cdot89 \times 30 = \mathbf{56\cdot7}.$$

To obtain the demand value for the building, for a given probability, the equation,

$$\text{demand} = \bar{x} + vs$$

is employed. For 95% satisfaction, the value of v, from Table 2.5 is 1·645, so

$$\text{demand} = 452\cdot7 + 1\cdot645(56\cdot8) = 546\cdot14$$

i.e., the designer should arrange to provide **547** dm^3 per day to satisfy 95% of the demand.

If three identical but independent buildings are to be supplied from the same source, the demand is given by the equation

$$
\begin{aligned}
\text{demand} &= N\bar{x} + \sqrt{(N)}vs \\
&= 3(452\cdot7) + \sqrt{(3)} \times 1\cdot645 \times 56\cdot8 \\
&= 1519\cdot7
\end{aligned}
$$

i.e., the designer should arrange to provide **1520** dm^3 per day to satisfy 95% of the demand in three identical buildings.

Problem

(3) Data on the growth in demand for natural gas in a factory complex over the last six years are given by the following table:

Number of years	1·1	1·9	3·5	4·8	5·4	6·1
Gas consumption: cubic metres/day	3·981	7·943	25·12	50·12	79·43	125·9

Estimate the daily consumption in two years' time.

Answer

Since it is required to estimate the consumption for a given point in time, consumption should be taken as the dependent variable, y, and time as the independent variable, x. The data, when plotted (Figure 2.9), show a rapidly increasing demand; if this is an exponential growth, the relationship between consumption and time will be:

$$y = ba^x$$

i.e., $\log y = x \log a + \log b$

which is linear in form. To check this, a plot can be made of x and $\log y$ (Figure 2.10) from which it is clear that a straight line fairly summarizes the data. It is now possible to proceed with the computation of the linear regression equation of $\log y$ on x:

y	3·981	7·943	25·12	50·12	79·43	125·9
$\log y$	0·6	0·9	1·4	1·7	1·9	2·1

x	$\log y$	$x \log y$	x^2	$(\log y)^2$
1·1	0·6	0·66	1·21	0·36
1·9	0·9	1·71	3·61	0·81
3·5	1·4	4·90	12·25	1·96
4·8	1·7	8·16	23·04	2·89
5·4	1·9	10·26	29·16	3·61
6·1	2·1	12·81	37·21	4·41
22·8	8·6	38·50	106·48	14·04

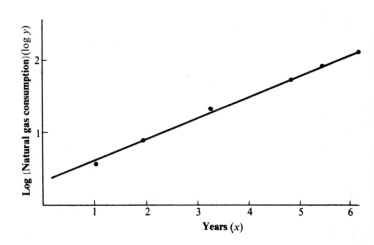

Figure 2.9

Now,

$$\log a = \frac{N\Sigma x \log y - \Sigma x \Sigma \log y}{N\Sigma x^2 - (\Sigma x)^2}$$

$$= \frac{6(38\cdot50) - (22\cdot8 \times 8\cdot6)}{6(106\cdot48) - (22\cdot8 \times 22\cdot8)} = \frac{40\cdot9}{119\cdot0} = 0\cdot344$$

$$\log b = \frac{\Sigma x^2 \Sigma \log y - \Sigma x \Sigma x \log y}{N\Sigma x^2 - (\Sigma x)^2}$$

$$= \frac{106\cdot48(8\cdot6) - (22\cdot8 \times 38\cdot50)}{6(106\cdot48) - (22\cdot8 \times 22\cdot8)} = \frac{37\cdot9}{119} = 0\cdot32.$$

Thus the straight line equation is

$$\log y = 0\cdot344x + 0\cdot32.$$

Alternatively,

if $\log a = 0\cdot344$, $a = 2\cdot208$
and $\log b = 0\cdot32$, $b = 2\cdot089$
i.e., $y = 2\cdot089(2\cdot208)^x$.

Now, in two years' time, $x = 8$
i.e., $y = 2\cdot089(2\cdot208)^8$
$= 1180$

i.e., an estimate of the daily consumption of natural gas in two years' time is **1180** cubic metres per day.

The drawing of the straight line is facilitated by the knowledge that it always passes through the point whose co-ordinates are the mean values of the variables, in this case

$(\bar{x}, \overline{\log y})$. Numerically, this point is

$\left(\dfrac{22\cdot8}{6}, \dfrac{8\cdot6}{6}\right)$ i.e., $(3\cdot8, 1\cdot43)$.

It is also known that the line intercepts the vertical axis at the point $(0, 0\cdot32)$. The line joining these two points is shown in Figure 2.10. The correlation coefficient can be computed from the expression

$$r = \frac{\Sigma x \log y - N\bar{x}\,\overline{\log y}}{\sqrt{\{\Sigma x^2 - N(\bar{x})^2\}}\sqrt{\{\Sigma(\log y)^2 - N(\overline{\log y})^2\}}}$$

and it is left to the reader to check that the value is close to $+1$.

3 Physical resources and laws

Energy sources and resources

Energy is defined as the physical ability to do work. Three main categories of resource are available; solar energy with an energy concentration of 1 kW/m^2; chemical energy with an energy-to-mass ratio of between 40 and 130 MJ/kg; and nuclear energy with an energy-to-mass ratio of 8×10^4 GJ/kg.

Nuclear energy
Energy is available from nuclear fission, fusion and radioactive decay. To date only nuclear fission is a practical proposition for the production of useful energy as heat.

Solar energy
Solar energy originates from the carbon cycle nuclear fusion reaction in the sun. Man is dependent on this energy for the production of fossil fuels, for the process of photosynthesis which provides him with food and for heat and light. Apart from the chemical energy contained in carboniferous fuels, the sun provides a source of mechanical energy by evaporating water from the sea which is then precipitated at high level with a consequent increase in potential mechanical energy. The practice of concentrating and storing the heat in the sun's rays has in some climates proved to be an economical proposition; attempts to directly convert sunshine into electricity by means of photo-voltaic cells or thermocouples are not yet viable.

Chemical energy
Energy derived from the oxidation of fossil fuels is the form most commonly used in the world now. (See Figure 3.1.)

Figure 3.1

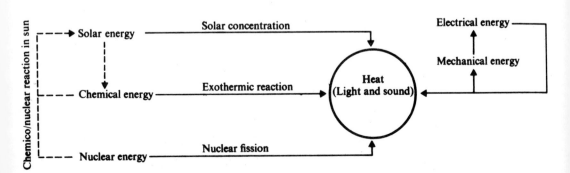

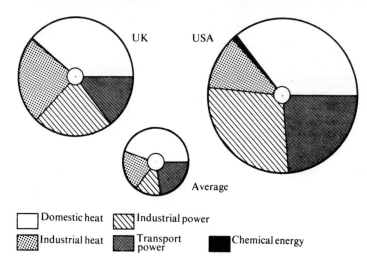

Figure 3.2

Domestic heat   Industrial power

Industrial heat   Transport power   Chemical energy

Energy conversion

Of direct interest to designers of engineering service systems are the facility and efficiency of converting from one energy form into another. Heat energy, mechanical energy and electrical energy are obtainable from the three main sources of energy as shown in Figure 3.1 and it will aid discussion of utilization and resources, if equivalence is established between them.

The efficiency of conversion from one energy form into another is, of course, dependent on the engine performing the transformation; whereas conversion from mechanical or electrical energy into heat energy can be achieved with efficiencies approaching 100%, the conversion from heat energy into mechanical or electrical energy is achieved with efficiencies approaching only 40%. It is necessary, therefore, in discussing energy utilization and resources to state clearly whether heat energy or electro-mechanical energy is meant.

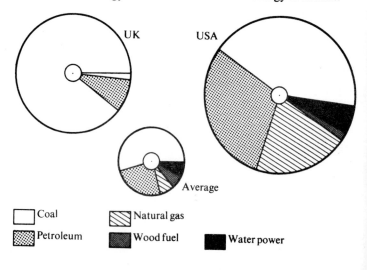

Coal   Natural gas

Petroleum   Wood fuel   Water power

Figure 3.3

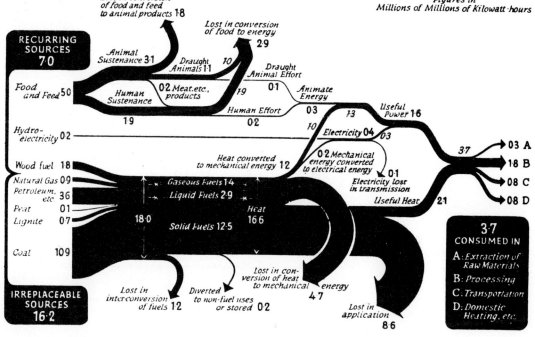

Figure 3.4
From: N. B. Guyol. (1949). *Energy
Resources of the World.* Department
of State Publication 3428. Washington,
DC, US Government Printing Office.

Energy utilization

Figure 3.2 gives the consumption *per capita* for various uses
and from various sources in the UK, USA and the world at
large during 1950. The inner circle is the *per capita* utilization
of animate energy per annum in terms of food consumption
and approximates to 3·6 GJ. Consumption *per capita* in
Figure 3.3 is in electricity equivalents with fuels taken at 20%
efficiency.

Comparison between the UK and other countries indicates
that in this country a high proportion of the energy consumed is from non-recurrent sources; in Norway, Sweden,
Switzerland and some other countries, a much higher proportion of the energy consumption is from replaceable fuel
reserves (wood, etc.) and water power. Figure 3.4 gives a
complete breakdown of the origin and utilization of the
world's energy in 1937.

Energy resources

The rise in global energy consumption in heat equivalents
over the last 200 years is shown in Figure 3.5; the lower
horizontal line shows the present annual output of energy
from recurrent sources and the upper horizontal line is an
estimate of the potential annual output, assuming full
development and optimum utilization. The demand curve has

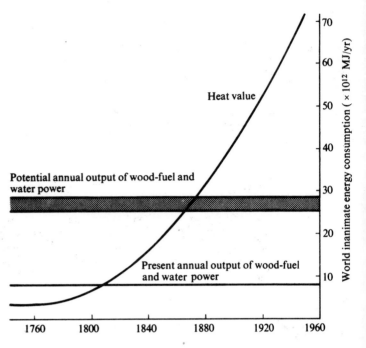

Figure 3.5

already crossed even the potential recurrent supply; with increasing population the rate of utilization of irreplaceable supplies will increase dramatically and it is pertinent to make some estimate of the limit of available resources.

Taking the best available estimates of growth in population and the growth *per capita* in energy demand available to him, Putnam[1] anticipates that mankind will have used up the available fossil fuels by AD 2025. While more recent projections[2] lead to a slightly more optimistic conclusion, it is, none the less, a sobering thought that buildings are at present being constructed to be in existence beyond this date.

Clearly, major efforts will be made to effectively harness solar and nuclear power, but there is every justification for examining means whereby the utilization and wastage of irreplaceable resources are reduced.

Other resources
Apart from his energy requirements, man must ensure the supply of fresh water and air, and the disposal of noxious wastes and pollutants, if his basic biological needs are to be satisfied. For fresh water, man depends mainly on the natural precipitation and storage of rain-water. At present, the annual *per capita* fresh water requirements of developing countries have been estimated at 1000 m^3; by the year AD 2000 the fresh water need of the world is predicted to be 5.9×10^{12} m^3/year. Although the theoretically utilizable

42

fresh water flow from all sources in the world is reckoned to be 6.36×10^{13} m³/year, the distribution of this flow over the earth's surface is such that many areas will still be short. Desalination of sea water is already a practical proposition in some areas of the world, but it is important to recognize the implications in relation to the energy investment. Silver[3] has observed that the ratio of water utilization to energy utilization in the USA and the UK has fallen from 126 dm³/MJ in 1930 to 12·6 dm³/MJ at the present time and that we are already pressing on diminishing resources; he argues that the lower limit of water/energy consumption is of the order of between 2·5 and 6 dm³/MJ, excluding water for agricultural use, to ensure basic standards of hygiene and health. Clearly, then, desalination plant must return an output of over 6 dm³/MJ to be viable.

The volume of oxygen in the world as a whole is, of course, extremely high, but, as with fresh water, certain areas have reached a level of pollution sufficiently high to jeopardize the natural supply. As *per capita* energy consumption rises the concentration of sulphur compounds and carbon dioxide in the atmosphere rises also. Further energy consumption may be necessary in densely populated areas to clean and filter the air taken into buildings.

A further problem in heavily populated areas is the effective disposal of solid and liquid waste. In the UK, the rate of production of liquid waste is growing at a rate of 2% per annum; by the year AD 2000 this means double the present quantity of sewage and industrial effluent. Over the past 20 years the volume of solid refuse collected has doubled and now stands at 76 million m³ a year (about 2 m³ per household per week); by AD 2000 the present volume will have doubled although the total weight will remain approximately at the present level – some 14 million tonnes. As the *per capita* energy needs and waste production increase, the pressure grows for the effective re-utilization of waste materials.

The laws of heat flow

Three distinct modes of heat flow will be considered.

Conduction
Thermal conduction is the flow within a body from an area of high heat energy to an area of low heat energy without displacement of the particles of the body.

The rate of transfer of heat $\dot{Q}$, over an area A, at right angles to the direction of flow from a surface at temperature

T_1 to a surface at temperature T_2, the surfaces being a distance d apart, is given by

$$\dot{Q} = \frac{kA(T_1 - T_2)}{d}$$

where k = the thermal conductivity of the body. The reciprocal, d/k, is termed the thermal resistivity.

If unit area is taken, the term k/d in the equation

$$\dot{q} = \frac{k}{d}\Delta T$$

is called the thermal conductance and is denoted by K, and the reciprocal d/k is called the thermal resistance and is denoted by R. Thus,

$$\dot{q} = K\Delta T$$

$$\dot{q} = \frac{\Delta T}{R}.$$

The latter of these two equations can be written

$$\Delta T = \dot{q}R$$

which is directly analogous, as we shall see, to the equation governing electrical flow, namely $V = IR$.

When heat is conducted through a number of interfacing materials, as in Figure 3.6

$$\dot{q} = \frac{T_1 - T_2}{R_{12}} = \frac{T_2 - T_3}{R_{23}} = \frac{T_3 - T_4}{R_{34}}$$

and $\quad \dot{q} = \dfrac{T_1 - T_4}{R_{14}}$

i.e., $R_{14} = R_{12} + R_{23} + R_{34}$.

Extending the electrical analogy, for materials in parallel, the total resistance is given by

$$1/R_{14} = 1/R_{12} + 1/R_{23} + 1/R_{34}.$$

Generally speaking, the thermal conductivity correlates positively with density; materials with low density, particularly with fibrous or granular structures containing air filled pockets, have low conductivity and provide the best insulation.

Figure 3.6

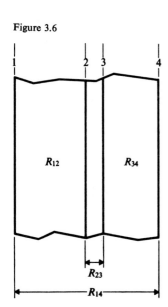

44

Convection

Convection describes the phenomenon whereby heat energy is transferred by fluid movement within a liquid or gas; movement is caused by the fact that the density of a fluid varies with temperature. In general, fluids become less dense with increase in temperature and warmer portions rise within a vessel to which heat is being applied.

The laws of heat flow by convection are complex, but a useful relationship describing the rate of heat flow between an area A of a heated surface and a fluid with which it is in contact is given by

$$\dot{Q} = hA(T_s - T_f)$$

where T_s = temperature of the heated surface,

$\quad\quad T_f$ = temperature of the fluid, and

$\quad\quad h$ = is defined as the surface coefficient of heat transfer or convection coefficient.

The coefficient h is not a constant in the normal sense but varies with the characteristics and velocity of the fluid flow over the heated surface, the temperature difference and the shape and proportions of the heated surface.

Radiation

The exchange of heat energy between two or more bodies by radiation is due to the transmittance of electromagnetic waves through a void or a medium which does not absorb them (e.g., air).

The equation of rate of heat flow radiating from a body is

$$\dot{Q} = Y\varepsilon AT^4$$

where Y = the radiation constant,

$\quad\quad \varepsilon$ = emissivity of the surface,

$\quad\quad A$ = area of the body, and

$\quad\quad T^4$ = temperature of the body, in absolute terms.

The value of Y is constant in all cases but the emissivity, ε, is dependent on the nature of the body and its temperature. The numerical value of ε ranges between zero and unity, being highest for black, non-metallic materials and lowest for materials such as highly polished aluminium.

Between the surfaces of two bodies, the net radiation heat transfer is given by

$$\dot{Q} = F_{12}F_{\varepsilon}A(T^4{}_1 - T^4{}_2)$$

where F_{12} = configuration factor which ranges between zero and unity and is dependent on the shape and relative position of the two bodies,

F_{ε} = emissivity factor which ranges between zero and unity and is dependent on the emissivity and absorptivities of the two bodies.

Steady state heat transfer

In the consideration of the transfer of heat from the fluid (indoor air) on one side of a membrane (wall) to the fluid (outdoor air) on the other side, an assumption regarding 'steady state' conditions simplifies the situation. Steady state assumptions are reasonable where the heat storing capacity of the membrane is small in relation to the total heat flow (lightweight construction) and where the temperature difference between the fluids is large in relation to the temperature fluctuations in either of the two fluids.

Figure 3.7 represents the temperature gradient between two fluids on either side of a composite membrane. Transfer of heat from fluid 1 to the surface of the membrane and from the other surface of the membrane to fluid 2 will be mainly by convection, whereas transfer within each part of the membrane and at the interfaces of the membrane will be mainly by conduction.

Figure 3.7

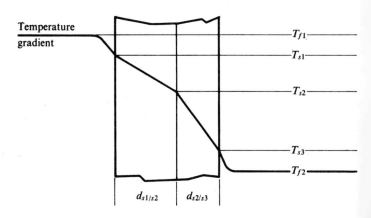

46

Now, since the rate of flow must be constant throughout (under steady state conditions),

$$\dot{Q} = h_{f1/s1}A(T_{f1}-T_{s1})$$

$$= \frac{k_{s1/s2}}{d_{s1/s2}}A(T_{s1}-T_{s2})$$

$$= \frac{k_{s2/s3}}{d_{s2/s3}}A(T_{s2}-T_{s3})$$

$$= h_{s3/f2}A(T_{s3}-T_{f2}).$$

If an overall coefficient of thermal transmittance, U, is taken, such that

$$\dot{Q} = UA(T_{f1}-T_{f2})$$

then,

$$U = \frac{\left(h_{f1/s1}\right)\left(\dfrac{k_{s1/s2}}{d_{s1/s2}}\right)\left(\dfrac{k_{s2/s3}}{d_{s2/s3}}\right)\left(h_{s3/f2}\right)}{h_{f1/s1}+\dfrac{k_{s1/s2}}{d_{s1/s2}}+\dfrac{k_{s2/s3}}{d_{s2/s3}}+h_{s3/f2}}$$

and the overall resistance, R, is given by

$$R = \frac{1}{h_{f1/s1}}+\frac{d_{s1/s2}}{k_{s1/s2}}+\frac{d_{s2/s3}}{k_{s2/s3}}+\frac{1}{h_{s3/f2}}$$

$$= R_{f1/s1}+R_{s1/s2}+R_{s2/s3}+R_{s3/f2}.$$

Variation with time

The specific heat of a substance is defined as the ratio of the quantity of heat required to raise the temperature of a given weight of the substance by a given amount to the quantity of heat required to raise the temperature of the same weight of water by the same amount. Thus, for a mass, m, of a substance with specific heat, c, the quantity of heat required to raise its temperature from T_1 to T_2 is given by

$$Q = mc(T_2-T_1).$$

The quantity mc is termed the thermal capacity of the substance.

Newton's law states that the cooling of a body at temperature T_1 immersed in a fluid at zero temperature proceeds according to the equation

$$\text{rate of cooling} = T_1 e^{(-\frac{h}{mc} t)}$$

where t represents time and h is the surface or convection coefficient. The rate of temperature increase of a body immersed in a warmer fluid is analogous. It can be seen that the rate of heating or cooling of a body is inversely related to its thermal capacity, mc. The quantity mc/h is called the thermal time constant.

Latent heat
When a substance changes its state without changing its temperature, there is a change in its thermal energy; the amount of this change is known as the latent heat, L, and is proportional to the mass of the substance. Thus,

$$L = ml$$

where l is the latent heat per unit mass.

The direction of the energy change is summarized as follows:

	heat in		heat in	
solid	$\xrightarrow{}$ $\xleftarrow{}$	**liquid**	$\xrightarrow{}$ $\xleftarrow{}$	**gas**
	heat out		heat out	

Structural implications
Under steady state conditions, the rate of heat flow through the envelope of a building can be computed from the equation

$$\dot{Q} = \Sigma U A (T_1 - T_2)$$

where U is the transmittance coefficient and A is the area of each part of the envelope, and T_1 and T_2 are the indoor and outdoor temperatures.

For design purposes, the minimum winter outdoor temperature would be considered in the estimation of the heating load, and the maximum outdoor summer temperature would be considered in the estimation of the cooling load. The value of the coefficient of thermal transmittance will depend on the conductance, convection and radiation characteristics of the fabric. It has been noted that the coefficient of thermal conductivity is lowest for fibrous and granular materials; the convection coefficient is lowest when the surface air velocity is minimized; and radiation emissivity is lowest when the surface has a high reflectance. Thus, the barrier presented to the flow of heat by a building envelope is most effective when it is thick, is fibrous, has a highly reflective surface, and the surface air velocity is low.

In real life, however, steady state conditions never prevail; the fluctuations in outdoor temperature in the UK are fairly rapid and the internal heat gains from equipment and people may also be variable. It is therefore necessary to consider the thermal capacity of the structure, mc. It is obvious that the greater the mass of the structure, the greater the thermal storage capacity, and, hence, the greater the effect the structure has in smoothing out the effects of temperature variation. For the stabilization of external changes in temperature it is relatively unimportant where, within a composite structure, the large mass is located: but where the source of variation is from within the building, the location of the large mass on the inside of the structure is more effective in maintaining a constant indoor temperature.

Apart from the transmittance of heat through the structure, flow of heat by ventilation through gaps in the structure and flow of heat by solar radiation through translucent elements must be considered in the sizing of heating and cooling plant. The rate of heat flow due to ventilation is given by

$$\dot{Q} = nVc(T_1 - T_2)$$

where V = volume of air inside the structure,
c = specific heat of air per unit volume,
n = number of complete changes of air in unit time,
$T_{1,2}$ = indoor and outdoor temperatures.

The heat gain due to solar radiation is related to the angle of incidence of the sun's rays to the plane of the glass. Throughout the year, east and west windows receive the sun's rays at near-normal incidence and gains are therefore high. For south-facing windows in the UK, the winter incidence is low and the summer incidence is high, therefore, solar heat gains may be greater during the winter months. Surfaces other than windows are subject, to a lesser extent, to solar heat gain, particularly if they are dark in colour.

The time variation in the indoor response to transmittance through the structure on the one hand and to ventilation and radiation flow on the other, makes accurate computation of the thermal performance of a building difficult. However, for the estimation of the output of a heating or cooling plant over a period of a year some empirical equations can be used. It is true to say that in any year

$$Q_I + Q_S + Q_P = Q_F + Q_V$$

where Q_I = total heat generated internally (by equipment, people, etc.),
Q_S = total heat from solar gains,
Q_P = total heat generated or removed by plant,
Q_F = total heat lost through the structure,
Q_V = total heat lost through ventilation,

i.e., $Q_P = Q_F + Q_V - Q_I - Q_S$.

It may be necessary to generate or remove heat only on certain days within a year. If, for any location, N is an estimate of the number of days when the heating plant will be in operation, then,

$$Q_P = 24\dot{Q}N\Delta T$$

where $\dot{Q}$ = hourly heat flow rate, and the product $N\Delta T$ is known as the number of 'degree days'.

This empirical relationship can be used for the estimation of total heat generated and, consequently, the fuel costs.

To determine heating or cooling plant size, however, the maximum output must be considered; if it is desired to heat or cool intermittently, the plant capacity will be many times greater than the average heating or cooling load. The basis for plant sizing thus relates to the thermal time response of the structure and the contents of the building.

Distribution implications
Distribution of heating or cooling from the installed plant to the required location may be by conduction, convection or radiation, by a mixture of any two or by all three. Where the plant is an open fire, the heat flows mainly by radiation; in large buildings with centralized plant, it is common to generate heat in, or remove heat from, a transfer medium, such as air or water and then to distribute this medium to locations where heating or cooling is required. A motive force may be applied to the medium, but as has already been noted, temperature differences within the medium will cause natural convection which may itself be sufficient to provide movement in the system.

The thermal capacity of media such as air, oil and water depends on the specific heat; the higher the specific heat, the greater the quantity of heat transferred per unit volume in unit time. The thermal capacity of steam, on the other hand, is dependent on the latent heat of condensation.

The heat transfer medium flows within a system of conductors – pipes in the case of water, steam and oil, ducts in the case of air – and control of the heat exchange from the heat transfer medium to the surrounds will depend on the nature of the conductor. Since thermal conduction is a function of area, the rate of flow of heat from a transfer medium through a pipe to the surrounds will be a function of the pipe diameter and length, and of the thickness and nature of the pipe wall. The rate of flow of heat caused by convection will also depend on pipe diameter and length, and on the velocity of fluid flow surrounding the pipe. The rate of heat flow caused by radiation will again depend on diameter and length, and on the nature of the outside surface of the pipe.

When it is desired to inhibit the flow of heat from a pipe, the diameter and length should thus be kept to a minimum, the pipe should be insulated with a material of high thermal resistance and a reflective surface, and flow of the surrounding fluid should be kept as low as possible. Conversely, when it is desired to promote heat flow, the transfer medium should be passed through a conductor which has as large a surface area as possible, is made of a material with a low thermal resistance and an unpolished black surface, and flow of the surrounding fluid should be kept as high as possible.

The laws of fluid flow

There are two basic energy states for systems which obey Newton's Laws of Motion: the potential energy state and the kinetic energy state. In fluid flow, the components of potential energy relate to the pressure of the fluid and the elevation of the container or conductor; the components of kinetic energy relate to the velocity of fluid flow in the conductor, to the energy input from a motive force and to the energy losses consequent on movement.

The energy exchange for a non-compressible fluid flowing in a pipe is represented in Figure 3.8. Bernoulli's equation, expressing the principle of energy conservation stated in the first law of thermodynamics can be written thus:

$$Z_1 + \frac{v_1^2}{2G} + \frac{P_1}{\rho} = Z_2 + \frac{v_2^2}{2G} + \frac{P_2}{\rho} + h_f$$

where Z = elevation above reference line,
v = velocity,
P = pressure,
ρ = density,
h_f = loss in head.

Where some motive force is applied to the fluid, e.g., by installing a pump in the pipeline, the additional head, h_p, would be recorded on the left-hand side of the energy balance.

It is important to note flow continuity is preserved in a full-flowing conductor, i.e., the fluid flow rate is constant. Thus,

$$\dot{V}_1 = \dot{V}_2$$
$$A_1 v_1 = A_2 v_2$$

where A_1 and A_2 are the cross-sectional areas at two points along the length of the conductor.

Figure 3.8

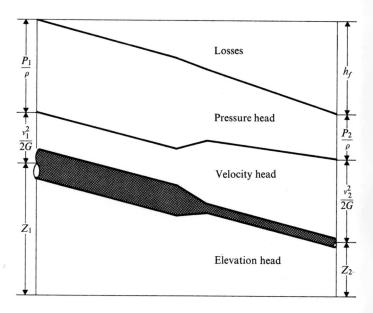

Head losses in pipes

Energy losses associated with fluid flow in pipes are mainly attributable to viscous-friction effects and to turbulent flow characteristics. Empirical expressions have been developed to estimate the viscous losses which may arise in a particular system, and the most useful equation is

$$\Delta h = \frac{l}{d} f \frac{v^2}{2G}$$

where Δh = head loss,
l = length of the pipe,
d = diameter of the pipe,
f = friction factor.

Other expressions have been developed to determine the head losses associated with sudden enlargements and contractions in pipe diameter, valves, bends, etc., and can be found in texts devoted to fluid mechanics.

Fluid networks

The principles governing flow in a fluid network (Figure 3.9) are analogous to these governing flow of current in an electrical circuit, i.e.,

(a) in any closed loop the algebraic sum of the pressure drops is zero,

(b) the algebraic sum of mass flows at any node is zero.

Analysis of the flow of fluids in a network is rather more difficult than the corresponding electrical analysis, since it has already been noted that the resistance to flow in any element of the network is dependent on velocity. None the less, the two general network principles are sufficient for the complete resolution of any problem.

Figure 3.9

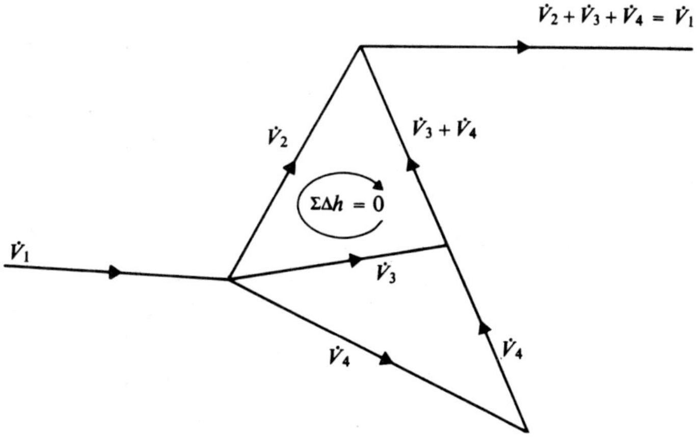

$$\dot{V}_2 + \dot{V}_3 + \dot{V}_4 = \dot{V}_1$$

$\dot{V}_2$

$\dot{V}_3 + \dot{V}_4$

$\Sigma \Delta h = 0$

$\dot{V}_1$

$\dot{V}_3$

$\dot{V}_4$

$\dot{V}_4$

Compressible fluids

Arising from the laws of Boyle and Charles, the general gas law can be defined, for an ideal gas, by the equation

$$\frac{P_1 V_1}{T_1} = \frac{P_2 V_2}{T_2}$$

where P_1, P_2 = initial and final pressure,
V_1, V_2 = initial and final volume, and
T_1, T_2 = initial and final temperature.

Most fluids, however, exist somewhere between the ideal non-compressible liquid and the ideal gas, and for these, a general form of equation for head loss can be expressed as:

$$\Delta h = F \frac{v^x}{d^y} \rho l$$

with F, x and y being determined experimentally for specific cases.

Distribution implications

From the equation giving the energy loss associated with fluid flow in pipes,

$$\Delta h = \frac{l}{d} f \frac{v^2}{2G}$$

it is clear that loss is reduced by having short runs of large diameter pipe with low velocity flow. It can also be seen from Figure 3.8 that the lower the destination point Z_2 in relation to the height of the source point Z_1 the lower will be the losses. Losses can be further reduced by keeping bends and sudden enlargements and contractions in the pipe to a minimum.

The quantity of fluid passing along a conductor in unit time, $\dot{V}$, was seen to be equal to the product of cross-sectional area, A, and the velocity, v. Increase in either velocity or area of cross-section will thus increase the fluid carrying capacity of the conductor.

The laws of electrical flow

Ohm's Law

The most basic law in electricity is due to Ohm and it can be stated: the resistance (R) to electrical flow in a conductor is equal to the voltage (V) applied between the ends of the conductor divided by the unit rate of flow in the conductor (I).

Thus,

$$R = \frac{V}{I}$$

where R = resistance in ohms,
V = voltage across the conductor in volts, and
I = rate of flow in amps.

The power generated by the flow of electricity is measured in watts (W) and is calculated from

$$W = VI = \frac{V^2}{R} = I^2 R.$$

Electrical energy is measured in joules (J); i.e., 1 watt for 1 second.

Electrical resistance
The resistance R is related to the characteristics of the conductor, thus,

$$R = K \frac{l}{A}$$

where l = the length of the conductor,
A = cross-sectional area of the conductor, and
K = constant dependent on the material of which the conductor is made.

In circuit, resistances may be connected in series or in parallel (Figure 3.10).

Figure 3.10

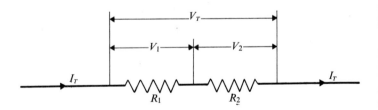

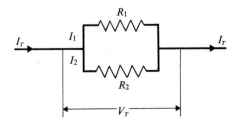

For series connected resistances, the current flowing in each section is the same, i.e.,

$$I_T = \frac{V_1}{R_1} = \frac{V_2}{R_2} = \frac{V_T}{R_T}.$$

Now, since

$$V_T = V_1 + V_2$$
$$I_T R_T = I_T R_1 + I_T R_2$$
$$\text{i.e., } R_T = R_1 + R_2.$$

For parallel connected resistances, the voltage across each section is the same, i.e.,

$$V_T = I_1 R_1 = I_2 R_2 = I_T R_T.$$

Now, since

$$I_T = I_1 + I_2$$

$$\frac{V_T}{R_T} = \frac{V_T}{R_1} + \frac{V_T}{R_2}$$

$$\text{i.e., } \frac{1}{R_T} = \frac{1}{R_1} + \frac{1}{R_2}$$

$$\text{i.e., } R_T = \frac{R_1 R_2}{R_1 + R_2}.$$

Electrical inductance and capacitance

An alternating current may be represented by a sinusoidal wave form with the amplitude measured in volts (Figure 3.11). The true value of voltage at any point in time is thus given by

$$V = V_{max} \sin \theta$$

$$\text{or } V = V_{max} \, \omega t$$

where t = time elapsed and ω = angular velocity in radians per second.

Figure 3.11

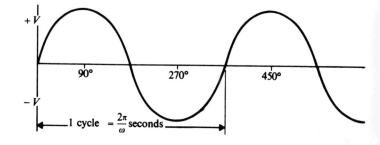

+V

90°   270°   450°

−V

1 cycle $= \dfrac{2\pi}{\omega}$ seconds

Figure 3.12

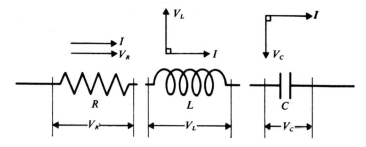

When current passes through a purely resistive circuit the relationship $I = V/R$ is true. Most circuits, however, have an inductive element and a capacitive element as well as a resistive element, and in this case, the relationship of current to voltage is more complex.

The phase relationship between current and voltage for resistive, inductive and capacitive circuits is represented in Figure 3.12. In the resistive circuit the current and voltage are in phase and $V_R = IR$; in the inductive circuit the current lags the voltage by 90° and $V_I = IL\omega\angle 90°$; in the capacitive circuit the current leads the voltage by 90° and

$$V_C = \frac{I}{C\omega} \angle -90°.$$

When these three elements exist together in a circuit (Figure 3.13) the voltage vector diagram is as shown in Figure 3.14. By Pythagoras,

$$V^2 = V_R{}^2 + (V_L - V_C)^2$$

$$\text{i.e., } (ZI)^2 = (RI)^2 + \left(L\omega I - \frac{1}{C\omega}I\right)^2 \tag{1}$$

where Z is termed the impedance of the circuit.

From (1)

$$Z = \sqrt{\left\{R^2 + \left(L\omega - \frac{1}{C\omega}\right)^2\right\}}.$$

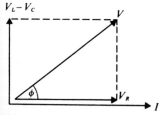

Figure 3.14

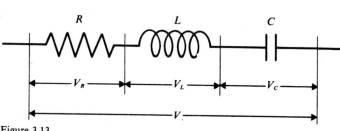

Figure 3.13

57

In this particular case, the resultant voltage leads the current which is given by

$$I = \frac{V}{\sqrt{\left\{R^2 + \left(L\omega - \frac{1}{C\omega}\right)^2\right\}}} \angle -\phi.$$

Considering the current vector diagram (Figure 3.15), it is clear that if the current lags the voltage by ϕ, the component of current in phase with voltage is $I \cos \phi$. Only this component contributes to the power generated which is therefore given by

$$W = (VI \cos \phi).$$

The product VI is evaluated in volt-amps (VA) and the product $VI \sin \phi$ is evaluated in volt-amps reactive (var). Cos ϕ is known as the power factor.

Losses in conductors
Consequent on the flow of electricity in a conductor is the drop in voltage along the conductor (cf. fluid flow losses on page 53). This loss is accounted for by a temperature rise in the conductor. The heat produced is given by

$$Q = \text{power} \times \text{time} = Wt = \frac{V^2}{R} t.$$

Electrical networks
The laws governing the flow of electricity in a network are analogous to those relating to fluid flow and were put forward by Kirchhoff. Kirchhoff's first law states that the sum of all the currents flowing towards a junction is equal to the sum of all the currents flowing away from the junction.

Figure 3.15

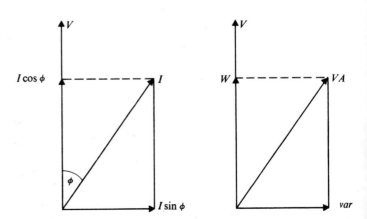

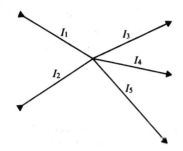

Figure 3.16

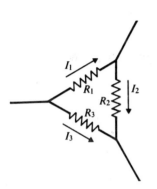

Figure 3.17

Referring to Figure 3.16 the law gives:

$$I_1 + I_2 = I_3 + I_4 + I_5.$$

The second law states that the voltage drop round any closed loop in the network is zero. Referring to Figure 3.17 the law gives:

$$R_1 I_1 + R_2 I_2 - R_3 I_3 = 0.$$

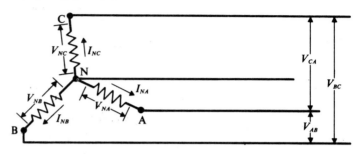

Figure 3.18

Polyphase distribution

Consider voltages V_{NA}, V_{NB} and V_{NC} relative to a neutral point N produced across resistances NA, NB and NC, as shown in Figure 3.18, such that the phase differences between voltage is 120° (Figure 3.19).

Then $V_{AB} = V_{NA} - V_{NB}$.

The vector diagram giving V_{AB} is thus as shown in Figure 3.20.

If $V_{NA} = V_{NB}$, then $V_{AB} = \sqrt{(3)}\, V_{NA} = \sqrt{(3)}\, V_{NB}$.

Similarly, if $V_{NC} = V_{NA} = V_{NB}$, the following relationships hold:

$$V_{AB} = \sqrt{(3)}\, V_{NA} = \sqrt{(3)}\, V_{NB} = \sqrt{(3)}\, V_{NC}$$
$$= V_{BC}$$
$$= V_{CA}.$$

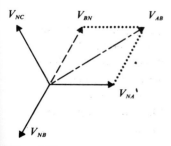

Figure 3.20

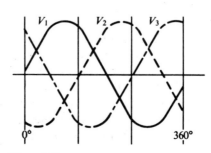

Figure 3.19

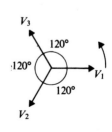

59

In general, denoting connections between the neutral point N and any other point by 'phase' connections and connections between any two points other than N as 'line' connections, it can be stated

$$V_{\text{line}} = \sqrt{(3)}\ V_{\text{phase}}.$$

Assume that the system is experiencing a balanced load, i.e., the phase voltages are numerically equal and are at 120° to each other and the phase currents are numerically equal and are at 120° to each other. Then, the total power in the system, W, is given by

$$W = 3 \times \text{power per phase}$$
$$= 3 \times V_{\text{phase}}\ I_{\text{phase}}\ \cos\phi$$

where ϕ is the phase difference between voltage and current in each of the phases.

Thus,

$$W = 3 \times \frac{V_{\text{line}}}{\sqrt{3}}\ I_{\text{line}}\ \cos\phi$$
$$= \sqrt{(3)}\ V_{\text{line}}\ I_{\text{line}}\ \cos\phi.$$

Distribution implications
The flow of electricity in a conductor is accompanied by a voltage drop which results in heat being produced. The drop in voltage is proportional to the resistance in the circuit, which is given by

$$R = \rho\frac{l}{A}.$$

Voltage drop will thus be reduced by keeping the length of the electrical cable short and the diameter large.

The capacity of an electrical current to do work is given by the equation

$$W = VI \cos\phi.$$

Since the power factor, $\cos\phi$, varies between 1 and 0 as ϕ varies between 0° and 90°, the power is maximized when voltage and current are in phase. When the current lags the voltage, extra capacitance may be added to the circuit to improve the power factor; when the current leads the voltage, extra inductance may be added to improve the power factor. The amount of capacitance required to effect a

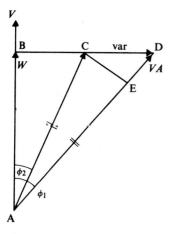

Figure 3.21

change in the power factor from $\cos \phi_1$ to $\cos \phi_2$ is readily calculated from Figure 3.21.

$$\text{The capacitance added} = BD - BC$$
$$= W \tan \phi_1 - W \tan \phi_2$$
$$= W(\tan \phi_1 - \tan \phi_2).$$

$$\text{The corresponding change in VA} = AD - AE$$
$$= AD - AC$$
$$= W \frac{1}{\cos \phi_1} - W \frac{1}{\cos \phi_2}$$
$$= W \left(\frac{1}{\cos \phi_1} - \frac{1}{\cos \phi_2} \right).$$

In 3-phase working, a balanced load is defined as one in which the phase voltages are equal and the phase currents are equal; under these conditions the current in the neutral line is zero. When the loads are unbalanced, current flows along the neutral line. To keep the sizing of the neutral line to a minimum, therefore, the loading applied to each phase should be as equitable as possible.

The laws of energy conversion and storage

Thermochemical exchange

Fossil fuels, the primary energy source in the world at the present time, are complex hydrocarbon compounds existing in solid (coal), liquid (oil) and gaseous (natural gas) states. When fuel burns in air the carbon is oxidized to carbon dioxide with the consequent output of heat, and the reaction is termed exothermic. The change of state of a compound from solid to liquid or from liquid to gas is also exothermic, the latent heat of fusion and evaporation being output as energy.

Endothermic reactions, on the other hand, are those changes of chemical or physical state accompanied by an intake of heat.

The exchange can be written thus:

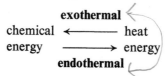

Energy can thus be stored in the form of chemical compounds or by collecting the heat energy resulting from a chemical reaction in a suitable medium which will exist at a temperature above or below that of its surrounds. The energy loss from chemical compounds is effectively zero while the rate of loss from a mass at temperature T_1 in surrounds at temperature T_2 is given by

$$(T_1 - T_2)e^{\left(-\frac{h}{mc}t\right)}.$$

Thermodynamic exchanges
The general gas law was previously stated as

$$\frac{P_1 V_1}{T_1} = \frac{P_2 V_2}{T_2}.$$

It follows that, in a constant pressure system, an increase in temperature will result in an increase in volume, which in turn implies motion. The most common example of a 'heat engine' is the internal combustion engine: ignition of fuel which is at a high pressure produces heat which produces an increase in volume and the piston is moved in the cylinder. Another example is the gas turbine in which the force provided by the volumetric increase of the burning gas is directly converted in rotary movement of the turbine blades, without the reciprocating linkage which typifies the internal combustion engine.

Heat energy can be converted into mechanical energy without combustion taking place, however, as the steam engine and the pure air engine demonstrate. The principle of operation is:
(a) the compression of the gas or vapour,
(b) the addition of heat,
(c) the expansion of the gas or vapour,
(d) the conversion of the expansion force into movement.

The operation of a heat engine is subject to the second law of thermodynamics, which means that the maximum efficiency theoretically possible is given by

$$\eta = \frac{T_1 - T_2}{T_1}.$$

Since the cycle can only operate by 'throwing away' heat at temperature T_2, the ideal of 100% efficiency cannot be achieved. Methods of using the rejected heat to assist in raising the temperature of the gas or vapour are employed in practice, but it is only with the greatest difficulty that efficiences of around 40% are realized.

If the heat engine cycle is reversed, i.e., mechanical work is applied to a gas, the result is an increase in heat energy in the gas. Such an arrangement is known as a 'heat pump' of which the compression refrigerator is a specific example. In the case of the refrigerator, the main objective is to remove heat from a substance with little regard to utilization of the heat energy gained; in the case of heat pumps generally, however, the prime interest is in heat energy produced for useful ends.

The theoretical 'efficiency' of the heat pump, known as the performance energy ratio (p), is, as would be expected, the reciprocal of the heat engine efficiency, i.e.,

$$p = \frac{T_1}{T_1 - T_2}.$$

Whereas increase in efficiency of the heat engine is related to increase in temperature difference, the opposite holds for the heat pump, i.e., efficiency increases with decrease in temperature difference.

The general statement of thermodynamic exchange can be expressed thus:

       heat engine
heat   ───────→ mechanical
energy ←─────── energy
       heat pump

The storage of heat energy has already been discussed. The storage of mechanical kinetic energy can be achieved (other than by conversion into heat or electricity) only by conversion into potential energy and subsequent re-conversion into kinetic energy. The exchange systems, such as the pumping of water to high level or the compression of a spring, have inherent inefficiencies due mainly to heat energy which is dissipated in the process. These losses are a further example of the conversion of mechanical energy into heat energy.

Electromechanical exchange
When a conductor is moved across a magnetic field, an electromotive force is produced in the conductor and current flows along it. This principle is employed in the generation

of electrical energy from mechanical energy, which can be achieved with efficiencies of over 90%.

When an electrical current flows through a conductor sited in a magnetic field, the conductor is subjected to a force which can be translated into mechanical energy. This phenomenon which is the complement of that dealt with above, is the basis of operation of the electric motor which converts electrical energy into mechanical energy. As with the generator, the efficiency of conversion may approach 100%.

Electromechanical exchange may be stated thus:

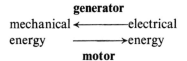

Storage of electrical energy, other than by conversion to, and subsequent reconversion from, another form of energy is not a practical proposition.

Thermoelectrical exchange
It has already been noted that when a current passes through a conductor the voltage drop in the circuit is transformed into heat energy. It is thus possible by incorporating a suitable resistance in an electrical circuit to generate heat in the substance surrounding the resistance. The efficiency of conversion can, in practice, approach 100%.

An alternative means of converting electrical energy into heat energy is by means of a bi-metal circuit. If a direct current is passed through the circuit in Figure 3.22, made up of metals A and B, the temperature at one junction becomes hot while the temperature at the other junction becomes cold. This phenomenon operates in reverse: i.e., if heat is supplied to one junction and removed from the other junction, direct electric current will flow round the circuit.

The exchange can thus be summarized:

electrical ⟵——— heat
energy ———⟶ energy

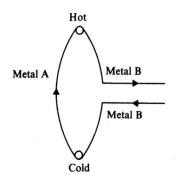

Figure 3.22

4 The economic laws of supply and distribution

Cost price and value

Money has two distinct functions: as a medium of exchange and as a standard unit of value. At a national level the UK buys certain commodities and sells others to various countries in the world; when a purchase is made, money is given in exchange and when a sale is made, money is received in exchange. The value of the purchases and sales made are measurable in terms of the amount of money exchanged.

It is easy to imagine situations in which the 'price' of an item or a service is the amount of money which it is necessary to exchange for the item or service, is not the same as the 'value' of the item or the service: the thirst-crazed man lost in the desert will consider a beer priced at £0·50 in the first village he reaches exceptionally good value whereas he will consider the same item at the same price very poor value the morning after an evening when he has consumed several over the eight in his 'local'. Those who produce items or services are not in a position, however, to have specific knowledge of the needs of every individual and they elect to set the price of whatever they are offering at a value which they estimate is appropriate to the 'market', i.e., to the average purchaser. In this 'open market' situation, price and value can be taken as synonymous; to avoid confusion, the word 'cost' will be defined in this text as the price or value of an item, commodity or service in the open market, i.e., when price and value are equal.

Consider an individual who earns £30·00 per week. In a single year he has, after deduction of taxes etc., a purchasing power of, say, £1,000·00; this he can apportion as he chooses between food, shelter, clothing, drink, transport, entertainment, etc. If he elects to spend 10%, i.e., £100·00 on entertainment, he can further apportion this amount as he chooses between the theatre, the cinema, night-clubs, etc. The economic alternatives open to him are exceedingly wide but, since he cannot exceed his total revenue of £1,000·00 and still be financially viable, he must recognize that the more he spends on night-clubs, the less he can spend on other entertainments and the more he spends on entertainment the less he can spend on food, shelter, clothing, drink and transport.

The financial operation of a commercial organization, or indeed of the government itself, is analogous to that of the individual. Revenue from the profits of commerce can be apportioned among the stockholders, the employees, the investment in new plant, the investment in new buildings, etc. Revenue from gross national production can be apportioned among health and welfare, education, defence, roads, etc.

Cost control

In a large organization it is common to institute a system of cost control based on the hierarchy of responsibility within the organization. Thus, the directors of the organization make an initial apportionment of the budget between, say, marketing, distribution, wages, dividends and new plant. Members of the organization are given responsibility for each of these functions and have control over the expenditure of funds up to the limit laid down for that particular function. The man responsible for new plant may elect to devote half his budget to new machinery and half to a new building, and to appoint a member of staff responsible for each. Thus the architect, commissioned to design a new warehouse, starts discussion with a representative of the organization who has at his disposal a limited amount of money. In some cases, apportionment of investment in building goes even further. Not only is there a limit to the total sum available, but the apportionment between different aspects of the building, e.g., 10% on substructure, 40% on structure, 20% on services, 20% on finishes, 10% on fittings, may be determined before the architect is appointed. Cost control by the specification of upper limits has some worrying features:

(a) in a probabilistic world a single definitive value is not the best way of specifying a cost limit; a mean and standard deviation would be more honest and more appropriate (as should be apparent from Chapter 2).
(b) since the fee structure for architects and consultants is based on a percentage of the cost of the building, there is no incentive, to say the least of it, to keep the cost of the building below the predetermined limit (a professional matter, beyond the scope of this book).
(c) limits for the building as a whole or for aspects of it tend to be decided on the cost analysis for previous buildings; the effect, therefore, is to progressively stifle innovatory solutions (which should be obvious).
(d) limits are set for initial capital expenditure only; this may preclude a design solution which, although initially more expensive, is cheaper when running costs and

maintenance costs are considered over the life of the building (see 'Cost-in-use' below).

(e) as with any investment, the amount invested may not be linearly related to the expected return; thus a 1% increase in investment over the present limit could result in a 50% increase in the performance of the building (see 'Cost and benefit', page 72).

Cost-in-use

As man has an expanding set of desires, it follows that there are never enough resources to satisfy them. The individual, the commercial organization or the government may try to belie this sad truth by borrowing money now to pay for what otherwise could only be afforded at some future time. The price to be paid for having 'future' money now is the interest payable on the borrowed capital. Clearly, then, the value of money varies with time.

The equations relating 'present' sums of money, 'future' sums of money and the annual equivalent of both are based on the laws of compound interest.

Let i = compound interest rate per year,

$\quad n$ = number of years,

$\quad C_P$ = present sum of money,

$\quad C_F$ = future sum of money, (n) years from the present,

$\quad C_A$ = a uniform annual payment at the end of each year.

Single payment present worth factor, $\left(\dfrac{C_P}{C_F}\right)$:

given a sum of money C_F, n years in the future, the present worth C_P is given by

$$C_P = C_F\left\{\frac{1}{(1+i)^n}\right\}.$$

Single payment compound amount factor, $\left(\dfrac{C_F}{C_P}\right)$:

given a sum of money C_P today, its future worth C_F, n years in the future is given by

$$C_F = C_P\{(1+i)^n\}.$$

Uniform annual present worth factor, $\left(\dfrac{C_P}{C_A}\right)$:

given the uniform annual amount C_A, the present worth C_P of these payments over a period of n years is given by

$$C_P = C_A\left\{\frac{(1+i)^n - 1}{i(1+i)^n}\right\}.$$

Uniform annual capital recovery factor, $\left(\dfrac{C_A}{C_P}\right)$:

given a sum of money C_P today, the uniform annual payment C_A to recover this capital cost over the next n years is given by

$$C_A = C_P\left\{\frac{i(1+i)^n}{(1+i)^n - 1}\right\}.$$

Uniform annual sinking fund factor, $\left(\dfrac{C_A}{C_F}\right)$:

given the sum of money C_F, n years in the future, the uniform annual payment C_A necessary to provide this money is given by

$$C_A = C_F\left\{\frac{i}{(1+i)^n - 1}\right\}.$$

Uniform annual compound amount factor, $\left(\dfrac{C_F}{C_A}\right)$:

given the uniform annual payment C_A for n years, the future sum of money C_F it will provide is given by

$$C_F = C_A\left\{\frac{(1+i)^n - 1}{i}\right\}.$$

Table 4.1 gives the value of the factors within the brackets for $i = 6\%$ and $n = 1$ to 60 years. Values for other interest rates are given in Table 2 of *Mathematics of Finance*.[1]

The equations given facilitate the comparison of the true cost of alternative design solutions which, it shall be assumed, satisfy the design requirements equally well. Either the recurring annual costs can be converted into present worth and added to the capital cost, or the capital cost can be converted into uniform annual costs and added to the

Table 4.1

n	$\dfrac{C_P}{C_F}$	$\dfrac{C_F}{C_P}$	$\dfrac{C_P}{C_A}$	$\dfrac{C_A}{C_P}$	$\dfrac{C_A}{C_F}$	$\dfrac{C_F}{C_A}$
1	0·943	1·06	0·94	1·060	1·000	1·00
2	0·890	1·12	1·83	0·545	0·485	2·06
3	0·840	1·19	2·67	0·374	0·314	3·18
4	0·792	1·26	3·47	0·289	0·229	4·38
5	0·747	1·34	4·21	0·237	0·177	5·69
6	0·705	1·42	4·92	0·203	0·143	6·98
7	0·665	1·50	5·58	0·179	0·119	8·39
8	0·627	1·59	6·21	0·161	0·101	9·90
9	0·592	1·69	6·80	0·147	0·087	11·49
10	0·558	1·79	7·36	0·136	0·076	13·18
15	0·417	2·40	9·71	0·103	0·043	23·28
20	0·312	3·21	11·47	0·087	0·027	36·79
25	0·233	4·29	12·78	0·078	0·018	54·87
30	0·174	5·74	13·77	0·073	0·013	79·06
35	0·130	7·69	14·50	0·069	0·009	111·40
40	0·097	10·29	15·05	0·066	0·006	154·70
45	0·073	13·77	15·46	0·065	0·005	212·70
50	0·054	18·42	15·76	0·063	0·003	290·40
60	0·030	33·33	16·16	0·062	0·002	538·83

recurring annual costs. Costs which may be pertinent are:
single sums:
Initial capital cost, replacement cost, salvage value.
recurring sums:
Fuel cost, maintenance cost, insurance cost, tax allowance.

Example

Two alternative heating systems are under consideration and details of the relevant costs are given. Assuming that the current rate of interest is 6%, compare the present worth of the alternatives. Check the answer by comparing the uniform annual equivalent costs.

	Scheme A	Scheme B
Capital cost	£20,000	£40,000
Life	20 years	30 years
Annual running and maintenance costs	£4,000	£2,000
Annual tax allowances	−£400	−£500
Salvage value	−£1,000	−£2,000

Present worth (taking a 60-year period)	Scheme A	Scheme B
Capital cost	£20,000	£40,000
Present worth of first renewal $= (\text{capital cost} - \text{salvage}) \times \left(\dfrac{C_P}{C_F}\right)$	£19,000 × 0·312 = £6,612	£38,000 × 0·17 = £6,460
Present worth of second renewal $= (\text{capital cost} - \text{salvage}) \times \left(\dfrac{C_P}{C_F}\right)$	£19,000 × 0·097 = £1,843	−
Present worth of annual running and maintenance costs $= (\text{annual cost}) \times \left(\dfrac{C_P}{C_A}\right)$	£4,000 × 16·161 = £64,644	£2,000 × 16·161 = £32,322
Present worth of annual fuel costs $= (\text{annual cost}) \times \left(\dfrac{C_P}{C_A}\right)$	£1,000 × 16·161 = £16,161	£2,000 × 16·161 = £32,322
Present worth of annual tax allowance $= (\text{annual amount}) \times \left(\dfrac{C_P}{C_A}\right)$	−£400 × 16·161 = −£6,464	−£500 × 16·161 = −£8,080
Present worth of final salvage value $= (\text{salvage value}) \times \left(\dfrac{C_P}{C_F}\right)$	−£1,000 × 0·030 = −£30	−£2,000 × 0·030 = −£60
Total present worth over 60 years	£102,082	£103,113

Thus, taken over a study period of 60 years, the present worth advantage of alternative A is £1,031.

Now, if the alternatives are compared in terms of uniform annual costs:

	Scheme A	Scheme B
Uniform annual equivalent of capital cost $= \text{(capital cost)} \times \left(\dfrac{C_A}{C_P}\right)$	£20,000 × 0·87 = £1,740	£40,000 × 0·073 = £2,920
Annual running and maintenance costs	£4,000	£2,000
Annual fuel costs	£1,000	£2,000
Annual tax allowance	− £400	− £500
Uniform annual equivalent of salvage value $= \text{(salvage value)} \times \left(\dfrac{C_A}{C_F}\right)$	− £1,000 × 0·027 = − £27	− £2,000 × 0·013 = − £26
Total annual equivalent	£6,313	£6,394

Thus the uniform annual cost advantage of alternative A is £81. The present worth of £81 over 60 years is given by £81 × 16·16 = £1,309 which checks with the figure already obtained, allowing for arithmetical inaccuracy.

Interest rates and life
The validity of a comparison between alternatives depends on the appropriate values being chosen for interest rate and life span. The interest rate selected should be the rate at which money could be borrowed to finance the scheme or the rate which could be achieved if money were invested in another project of equal risk. Any change in interest rate over the study period is likely to be accompanied by a change in costs and, since the designer's decision is based on a comparison of costs rather than on absolute costs, the outcome is not seriously affected. Incorrect estimation of the life span of alternative schemes is more serious, although the effect diminishes rapidly for lives over 20 years.

It can be argued that in an uncertain world there is an inherent advantage in a solution with a short life span, as it can be replaced sooner with a scheme more suited to a set of changed requirements. Against this it can be said that seldom is a scheme which has reached the end of its effective life actually replaced due to the failure to make suitable financial provision for the replacement; instead, grossly inefficient plant is allowed to soldier on.

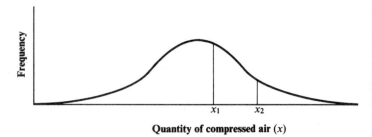

Figure 4.1

Quantity of compressed air (x)

Cost and benefit

In the foregoing section a method was proposed for comparing the cost of two alternative schemes which were capable of satisfying the design requirements equally well. In most cases, however, design decisions have to be made regarding a choice between alternative schemes, or between alternative levels of provision of a single scheme, when the performance characteristics of the alternatives are dissimilar.

Consider the demand for compressed air in a motor-car factory (Figure 4.1) which can be assumed to be normal with mean $\bar{x}$ and standard deviation s.

If the demand function in Figure 4.1 is plotted accumulatively, as in Figure 4.2, the vertical axis gives the probability of occurrence of a demand up to the value x. Thus the probability of a demand less than or equal to x_1 is given by P_1 and of a demand less than or equal to x_2 is given by P_2. It follows that if plant of size x_i is installed, P_i of the possible demand will be satisfied and $(1-P_i)$ of the possible demand will remain unsatisfied.

Figure 4.2

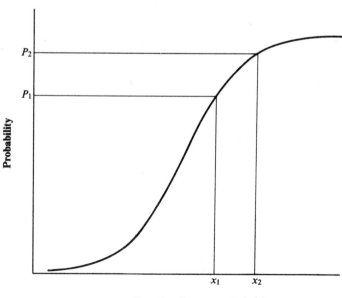

Quantity of compressed air (x)

Now on those occasions when the installed plant is inadequate to meet the demands, it is likely that production in the factory will be reduced. If loss in production can be costed, the relationship between the probability (or frequency) of success P and cost of failure can be plotted as in Figure 4.3. But since the relationship between x and P is known (Figure 4.2), Figure 4.3 can be redrawn using x as the horizontal axis (Figure 4.4). Thus, the cost of failure of the plant can be related to plant size.

By a simple costing exercise the cost of provision of the plant can be related to plant size x, as in Figure 4.5. When Figures 4.4 and 4.5 are combined (Figure 4.6), the total cost function exhibits a minimum, $£C_{to}$, at $x = x_o$. Thus, by giving consideration to the cost of provision of plant and the cost of failure incurred, the designer has been able to optimize the return on the client's monetary investment.

In the foregoing the concept of 'cost of failure' was introduced; it would have been equally reasonable to take the converse concept – that of benefit. In many design situations, the technique of cost-benefit analysis is employed in the search for an optimum design, but, as in the field of engineering service, the main problem is that of expressing benefit (or failure) in monetary terms. Failure of the electrical supply in one part of a hospital may result in nothing more than a degree of inconvenience; in the operating theatre suite, however, the consequences may be dire.

The translation of benefit or failure into cost terms requires considerable ingenuity, particularly in building types from which no recognizable unit of production emerges. A noteworthy example is an analysis of the effects of air condition-

Figure 4.3

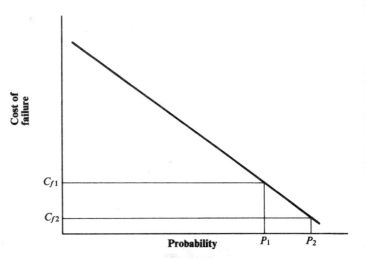

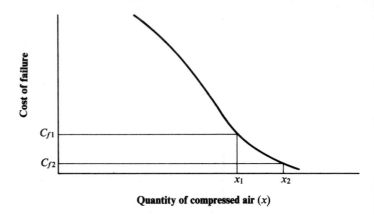

Figure 4.4

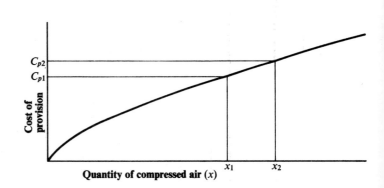

Figure 4.5

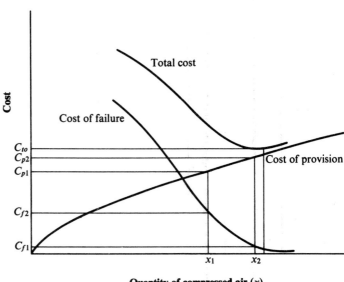

Figure 4.6

ing a chest disease ward in an urban hospital: the installation of air conditioning in a sample ward resulted in a reduction in the average length of stay of patients; since the capital cost and the cost per day of an occupied bed is known, the savings achieved in the treatment of a set number of patients over a set period of time is costable and can be compared with the cost of the air conditioning plant.

When the problem of quantifying the benefit gained from alternative solutions in cost terms is insurmountable, the designer should leave the decisions to the client. The alternatives may be demonstrated to the client in 'cost-effectiveness' terms, thus:
scheme A costs $£C_A$ and satisfies P_A of the demand;
scheme B costs $£C_B$ and satisfies P_B of the demand.

Multi-variate cost optimization

In the example on the sizing of compressed-air plant already described, an optimum plant size, x_o, at a cost $£C_{to}$, was determined. In like manner it may be possible to determine the optimum size and cost of the other services in the car factory. It is conceivable, however, that the cost limit set for the services as a whole is less than the sum of the individual cost minima. In this case the designer must have a method for the determination of the degree to which he ought to depart from the optimum solution relevant to each service.

Consider the case of the supply of compressed air in more detail (Figure 4.7). A departure from the optimum plant

Figure 4.7

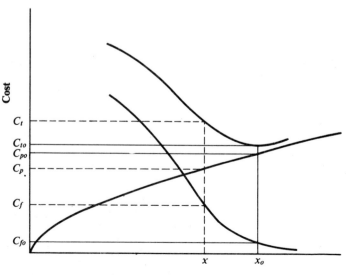

Quantity of compressed air (x)

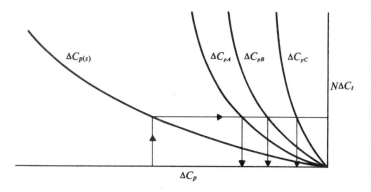

Figure 4.8

size, x_o, to a smaller installation, x, will result in new values of total cost C_t, cost of failure C_f and cost of provision C_p. The relationship between ΔC_p and ΔC_t can be described for the supply of compressed air, ΔC_{pA}, or for any other service under consideration, ΔC_{pB}, ΔC_{pC}, graphically as in Figure 4.8; the value of N in the expression $N\Delta C_t$ is unity if each service is considered separately. If ΔC_{pA}, ΔC_{pB} and ΔC_{pC} are now summed, $\Delta C_{p(s)}$, the corresponding value of $N\Delta C_t$ will be $3\Delta C_t$.

Assume now that from the original analysis of each service, as in Figure 4.6, the sum of the individual costs of provision for optimum conditions C_{poA}, C_{poB}, C_{poC} was £10,000 but that the cost of provision limit for the three services is £9,000. Then the value $\Delta C_{p(s)} = $ £1,000 can be read off from Figure 4.8 and the corresponding value of ΔC_{pA}, ΔC_{pB} and ΔC_{pC} noted. By reference to the relationships in Figure 4.6, the plant size for each service can be obtained.

The basic principle in the procedure just described is that of modifying individual optima according to the sensitivity of total cost to changes in the cost of provision. It should be obvious that increasing the amount of money available for plant beyond the sum of the individual cost-of-provision optima is wasteful and that sensible choice for a cost limit is ΣC_{po}.

Tariff structures in the UK

In the cost-in-use example described previously, some costs were associated with the initial provision of plant and some with the continuing operation of the plant. When energy or water is purchased from a supplier, it is common for the supplier to apply a tariff of charges which reflects his own investment in both initial provision and continuing operation. This section deals with the structure of energy and water tariffs in the UK, but it should be noted that since the market cost may be related to demand as well as supply, tariff structures are constantly under review.

Water

Water is purchased from the local water authorities and is charged, in premises which are metered, by consumption and in non-metered premises in proportion to the rateable value. Normally domestic premises are not metered but are charged at y new pence in the pound of their full rateable value; other premises which are not metered may be charged at y new pence in the pound if the full rateable value of the usage is predominantly domestic (e.g., hospitals, prisons, etc.), or at y new pence in the pound or some fraction (e.g., one-half) of the full rateable value if the usage is less than domestic usage (e.g., offices, shops).

In metered premises, it is common to have a flat rate of, say, £0·015 per 1000 dm^3 subject to a minimum quarterly charge based on meter size.

For building construction sites where the supply is not metered, a percentage rate based on the total contract price of the wet trades part of the total contract price may be levied. One example is ($\frac{1}{4}\%$) on the first £250,000 of the contract price, ($\frac{1}{8}\%$) on sums above £250,000.

Oil

Since oil is bought from commercial organizations rather than from public authorities, costs are negotiable in any particular situation. The oil companies quote a flat rate cost per dm^3 relating to different 'zones' in the UK, but will negotiate rebates based on the delivery load size and the proximity of the consumer to a supply depot. As with coal, the consumer can select from oils of differing quality and calorific value.

Gas

Town gas is purchasable from the local gas board. Domestic consumers normally qualify for either a general purpose block tariff – in which the price per 100 MJ or per volumetric measure is based on a diminishing series of rates applied to successive blocks of units supplied within a three-month period – or a two-part tariff – which consists of a fixed quarterly charge together with a block tariff or flat rate in which the unit costs are somewhat lower. Non-domestic users may or may not qualify for a two-part tariff, depending on the local gas board; some boards offer one or other of the two tariff structures with different unit rates to specialized consumers, e.g., bakers, public lighting authorities, industrial, catering, etc. Minor variations exist between boards in the details of the operation of the tariffs: fixed charges may be in relation to meter size; different zones in the area covered by the board may be charged at different unit rates.

In those areas where natural gas is supplied, the types of tariffs offered are similar to those for town gas, but the charges per 100 MJ are a little less.

Coal

The price of domestic coals, purchased through a merchant, depends mainly on the heat content of the coal but relates also to other factors such as the burning characteristics (free-burning, coking, etc.), ash content, appearance, etc. Domestic coals are sold on a delivered price basis and for this purpose the UK is divided up into 22 zones; the price difference from zone to zone reflects the transport costs incurred by the National Coal Board in supplying each zone. Four main grades of coal, designated A to D are available and the cost of any grade is constant within a zone.

Coal for non-domestic purposes is purchased either from a merchant or directly from the National Coal Board and price differentials operate according to type of consumer – gas works, industry and commerce, local authorities, hospitals, etc. Within the three main types of coal – bituminous, carbonizing and anthracitic – the pithead price is set according to such characteristics as ash content, size, sulphur content; to the pit price is added the appropriate transport costs. Although price does not depend on quantity taken, the National Coal Board is prepared to consider negotiating long-term contracts on special terms, where appropriate.

Electricity

Electricity may be purchased from the electricity board serving the area in which a new building is to be sited; sixteen electricity boards cover the UK and the tariff structure is different in each.

There are four basic tariff types:
(a) flat-rate tariffs which consist of a single charge proportional to the number of units supplied,
(b) block tariffs in which the price is based on a diminishing series of rates per unit applied to successive blocks of units supplied within a prescribed period; the blocks may be fixed or variable and assessed on floor area, number of rooms or installed load,
(c) maximum demand tariffs are constructed in two parts: a charge for total consumption and a charge for maximum demand occurring over 30 minutes within a prescribed period. Both parts may be 'blocked' as in (b) and

the rates per unit consumed tied to the magnitude of the maximum demand,

(d) off-peak tariffs in which any one of the tariff structures (a), (b) and (c) may be applied at a lower-than-normal unit rate to consumption occurring outside prescribed peak-load hours.

All electricity boards recognize two or more of the following consumer types: domestic, industrial, commercial, catering and agricultural.

Only certain of the tariffs may be offered to any particular type of consumer and then perhaps only if the demand falls between certain limits. On some tariffs an additional fuel cost variation charge is levied to take account of marginal charges in the cost and calorific value of the coal purchased by the supplier.

The complexity of most maximum demand tariffs is such that the designer may have considerable difficulty in comparing alternative electricity supply systems. Consider the following hypothetical but typical monthly maximum demand tariff for supplies metered at 650 V or less:

For the kilowatts of maximum demand at unity power factor:

for each of the first 200 kilowatts	£0·8375
for each of the next 800 kilowatts	£0·75
for each of the next 2000 kilowatts	£0·70
for each additional kilowatt	£0·625

For the units supplied:

for each of the first 200 units per kilowatt of maximum demand at unity power factor in that month	0·40416p
for each of the next 200 units per kilowatt of maximum demand at unity power factor in that month	0·3625p
for each additional unit	0·3p

Let $U=$ number of units consumed in kWh, $M=$ maximum demand in kW, and $K=$ constant. Then, assuming unity power factor,

for $M<200$
$$C_M = £0{\cdot}8375M \tag{a}$$

for $200<M<1000$,
$$C_M = £(200\times0{\cdot}8375)+£0{\cdot}75(M-200)$$
$$= £17{\cdot}5+£0{\cdot}75M \tag{b}$$

for $\dfrac{U}{M}<200$
$$C_U = (0{\cdot}40416U)\text{p}$$
$$= £0{\cdot}0040416U \tag{c}$$

for $200<\dfrac{U}{M}<400$
$$C_U = \{(200M\times0{\cdot}40416)+(U-200M)0{\cdot}3625\}\text{p}$$
$$= £0{\cdot}085M+£0{\cdot}003625U \tag{d}$$

for $400<\dfrac{U}{M}$
$$C_U = \{(200M\times0{\cdot}40416)+(200M\times0{\cdot}3625)+(U-400M)0{\cdot}3\}\text{p}$$
$$= £0{\cdot}3M+£0{\cdot}003U \tag{e}$$

Table 4.2

These results can be tabulated as in Table 4.2.

M range	$\dfrac{U}{M}$ range	Equations	Total monthly cost (£)		
			Kcost	Mcost	Ucost
	0–200	a+c		$0{\cdot}8375\ M$ +	$0{\cdot}0040416\ U$
0–200	200–400	a+d		$0{\cdot}92083\ M$+	$0{\cdot}003625\ U$
	400–	a+e		$1{\cdot}17073\ M$+	$0{\cdot}003\ U$
	0–200	b+c	$17{\cdot}5$ +	$0{\cdot}75\ M$ +	$0{\cdot}0040416\ U$
200–1000	200–400	b+d	$17{\cdot}5$ +	$0{\cdot}83\ M$ +	$0{\cdot}003625\ U$
	400–	b+c	$17{\cdot}5$ +	$1{\cdot}085\ M$ +	$0{\cdot}003\ U$

From this analysis the contribution to the price paid for electricity by the number of units consumed and by the level of the maximum demand is readily recognized.

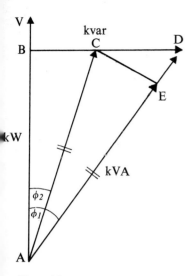

Figure 4.9

In the example given, the tariff related to consumption in kW; had the *Mcosts* been made against kVA, the level of the consumer's power factor would have been of considerable importance. In Figure 4.9 the reduction in kVA for a change in power factor from $\cos \phi_1$ to $\cos \phi_2$ is CD; the magnitude of capacitance which has been added is ED. Now, return on investment = benefit − cost

$$= \text{annual tariff saving} - \text{annual cost of capacitance.}$$
$$= \{12 \times (Mcost) \times CD\} - (\text{annual cost for one unit of capacitance} \times ED).$$

Assume a monthly load of $M = 180$ kVA, $U = 37\,000$ kWh and assume a capacitor costs £6 per unit of kvar and has a life of 15 years. Then, the *Mcost* per month = £0·92083M, from Table 4.2 and the annual capacitance cost
$= 0·103 \times £6 = £0·618$, from Table 4.1.

It has already been shown on page 61, that
$$CD = W(\tan \phi_1 - \tan \phi_2)$$

and $ED = W\left(\dfrac{1}{\cos \phi_1} - \dfrac{1}{\cos \phi_2}\right).$

Thus,

$$\text{return} = \{12 \times 0·92083 \times 180(\tan \phi_1 - \tan \phi_2)\}$$
$$- \left\{0·618 \times 180\left(\frac{1}{\cos \phi_1} - \frac{1}{\cos \phi_2}\right)\right\}$$
$$= 1944(\tan \phi_1 - \tan \phi_2) - 111\left(\frac{1}{\cos \phi_1} - \frac{1}{\cos \phi_2}\right).$$

By substitution for ϕ_1 and ϕ_2, the existing and proposed phase angles, an estimate of return can be obtained; thus if the existing power factor is 0·8 and it is proposed to improve it to 0·9, then,

$\cos \phi_1 = 0·8$, i.e., $\phi_1 = 36°52'$, i.e., $\tan \phi_1 = 0·7499$
$\cos \phi_2 = 0·9$, i.e., $\phi_2 = 25°50'$, i.e., $\tan \phi_2 = 0·4841$
i.e., return $= 1944(0·7499 - 0·4841) - 111\left(\dfrac{1}{0·8} - \dfrac{1}{0·9}\right)$

$$= £258 \text{ per annum.}$$

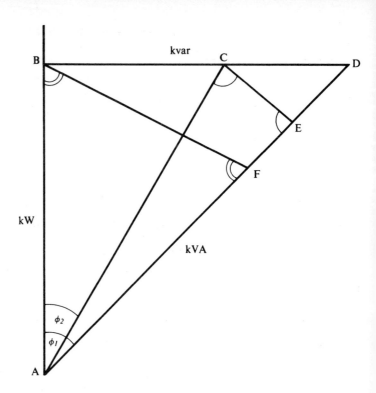

kvar

kW

kVA

ϕ_2

ϕ_1

Figure 4.10

The general case is best considered by reference to Figure 4.10. When the phase angle is changed to ϕ_2, the benefit is proportional to ED and the cost to CD; when the phase angle is changed to zero, the benefit is proportional to FD and the cost to BD. Clearly, the change in var is always greater than the change in VA, thus there is *never* a positive return on investment if the unit var cost is greater than the unit VA saving. When the unit var cost is less than the unit VA saving, the conditions for maximum return are given by

$$\frac{\text{unit VA saving}}{\text{unit var cost}} = \frac{\tan \phi_1 - \tan \phi_2}{1/\cos \phi_1 - 1/\cos \phi_2}.$$

Knowing both unit costs and ϕ_1, the value of ϕ_2 which will maximize return can be obtained by iterative approximations. For the limiting case, when ϕ_2 = zero, this expression becomes

$$\frac{\text{unit VA saving}}{\text{unit var cost}} = \frac{\tan \phi_1}{1/\cos \phi_1} = \tan \phi_1 \cos \phi_1 = \sin \phi_1.$$

Thus, there will *always* be a positive return if:

unit VA saving $>$ unit var cost $\times \sin \phi_1$.

5 Individual sub-systems

In this chapter, the main sub-systems which make up the engineering services in buildings will be dealt with individually and reference will be made to the relevance of the laws developed in previous chapters to their efficient design.

Hot and cold water services

Supply and distribution of hot and cold water are necessary in most buildings to ensure an adequate standard of hygiene of the occupants of the building, of the clothes, equipment and utensils used by the occupants and of the building fabric itself; closely associated with hygiene is the necessity of waste disposal which may be facilitated by adequate supplies of water. A requirement quite different in character from that of hygiene is for the means to contain and extinguish fires which otherwise could destroy the contents and fabric of the building. The third and most obvious requirement is that a supply of potable water should be available to satisfy the physiological needs of organic life within the building. In certain building types (e.g., laundries, breweries), water may be a prime commodity in the service or production process itself and in these cases special study would be required of the process operation.

A typical system
A typical system, in which it is assumed that a supply of water is available from the local water board at point A at a certain temperature and pressure, is shown in Figure 5.1;

Figure 5.1

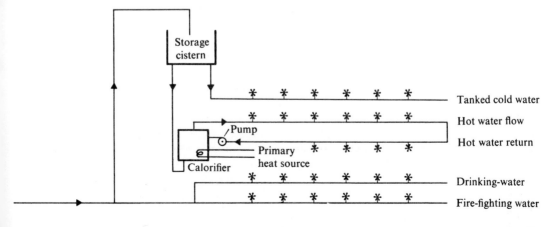

it is also assumed that heat is available from a primary heat source at point B. Cold water for drinking and cooking, and cold water for fire-fighting purposes may be piped directly (either together or separately as in Figure 5.1) to the locations where it is required. Cold water for other purposes may be stored, prior to distribution, in a cistern at high level. The calorifier, which is a heat exchange apparatus which may have provision for the storage of hot water, is fed from a high-level storage cistern; in all but the smallest building, the distribution of hot water is achieved by means of a pipe loop through which the hot water is circulated round the building from the calorifier, and returned to it using natural convection or a pump, as in Figure 5.1.

The following sub-sections deal with the main design variables in the system just described.

Storage cisterns

The provision of a storage cistern may be justified for one or more of the following reasons:

(a) it provides a 'buffer' against heavy instantaneous demand on the local authority main,

(b) it provides a reservoir in the event of the local authority supply failing,

(c) it prevents the back syphonage of polluted water into the local water board main, and,

(d) it provides a safety margin in the event of malfunctioning of the thermostat in the calorifier.

In most low-rise and medium-rise buildings the mains pressure is sufficient to overcome the elevation head and the losses in the pipe work in lifting water to the storage cistern; the efficient sizing of this pipework and of the cistern itself will depend on:

(a) the rate of demand for hot water and tanked cold water,

(b) the costs associated with the cistern and the pipework, and

(c) the physical laws of fluid flow.

As has already been noted, the demand for hot and cold water over time is variable. Assume that the demand over a critical period is shown in Figure 5.2; a possible rate of supply of water to the cistern from the local water board main could thus be represented by the line MN. From the time t_m onwards, the rate of demand is in excess of the rate of supply and this continues to the time t_y, after which the supply begins to catch up with the demand, until, at time t_n, the cycle is complete. The operation of a cistern with the supply rate MN, subject to the given demand, is represented beneath the graph in Figure 5.2. At time t_m the level in the cistern begins to fall and the ball-valve opens; the level continues to fall until time t_y is reached, after which the level beings to rise until the time t_n when the cistern is once again full and the ball-valve closes. Thus, for the given demand pattern and the given supply rate MN, the cistern must have had a capacity of at least XY cubic metres in order to cope with the demand.

Knowing the pressure of the supply point A, the height of the storage cistern and the required pressure at the ball valve, the size of the pipework between A and the cistern which will provide water at a rate MN, can be calculated using the laws of fluid flow established in Chapter 3. If the pipe size is known, it can be costed. Similarly the cost of a cistern of capacity XY can be obtained. The total cost of the system will be the sum of the pipework cost and the cistern cost.

Now, the foregoing analysis could have been performed assuming a supply rate different from MN. This would have resulted in a different cistern capacity, a different pipework cost and a different cistern cost and hence a different total cost. Clearly then, it is important to investigate a variety of supply rates to determine the most economic combination of pipework size and cistern size which will satisfy the demand.

For simplicity of explanation, the only variable which was considered as affecting the cistern cost was the size of the cistern itself. At this point however, it is important to begin

Figure 5.2

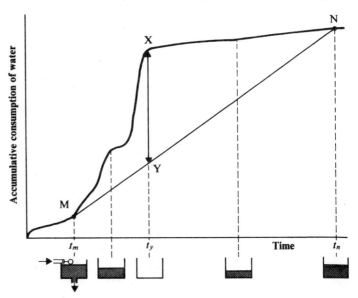

to identify the interaction between the engineering services and the other building systems. A cistern must be housed and it must be supported; the cost of the space occupied by the cistern and the cost of the structure required to support it, both positively correlated to the size of the cistern, must be taken into account in the design optimization procedure.

If the pressure in the local authority main is insufficient to lift the supply to a storage cistern at high level, a pump may be fitted on the supply side; in this case the economic analysis would have to take account of the initial and running costs of the pump. Other solutions, developed for high-rise buildings, include:

(a) the hydropneumatic tank situated at ground level in which water is stored in the lower half with a volume of air trapped above it; water is introduced into the tank by means of a pump which cuts in when the water level reaches a predetermined low point. The correct ratio of air to water is maintained by an air compressor. The system is designed such that the pressure in the tank is sufficient to supply water to the outlets within the building. The main economic trade-off which is relevant in this case is whether the additional expense of the pressure tank, pump and air compressor is less than the structural and spatial costs associated with the high level, non-pressurized storage.

(b) continuously running pumps sited on the discharge side of a non-pressurized storage tank at ground level. The pumps in this case must be sized to provide a flow equal to the maximum rate of demand. Again, an economic comparison can be made between this system, the hydropneumatic tank and the high-level cistern.

It was stated earlier that storage of water may be desirable as a means of obviating the consequences of a failure in the local authority supply. In certain areas there is a mandatory requirement to provide sufficient storage to meet demands over a given period of time, say 24 hours, but, if demand varies from day to day, it is not such a simple matter to determine what a 24-hour demand in fact is. If data on daily demand can be gathered however, the frequency distribution can be obtained and an analysis, similar to that outlined in Chapter 3, can be performed with the object of minimizing the total cost. The variables making up the total cost are:

(a) the cost of provision of storage, and

(b) the cost consequences of failure to meet the demand in the event of mains failure.

Calorifiers

The operation of a hot water calorifier can be taken as being analogous to the operation of a storage cistern: the variable output of hot water caused by demand must be met by the supply input of cold water and of heat. The traditional pattern of calorifier is shown in Figure 5.3. Cold water enters at the bottom of the vessel close to the source of heat; when the cold water is raised in temperature it moves by the laws of convection to the top of the vessel from where it may be drawn off. At periods of heavy demand the proportion of hot water to cold water in the vessel will be low; as demand reduces, the proportion of hot water to cold water will increase until the vessel is full of hot water. The thermostat, which controls the supply of heat, is analogous to the ball-valve in a cistern; when demand occurs, the level of cold water rises, the thermostat senses this and the supply of heat commences; when the vessel fills again with hot water, the thermostat senses this and cuts off the supply of heat. Figure 5.3 shows a definitive interface between the hot water and the cold water in the vessel; in practice, the degree to which this interface is defined depends mainly on the speed of inflow of cold water and on the temperature difference between the hot and cold water.

The main design variables are the storage volume of the calorifier and the size of the heating element. Figure 5.4 shows the operation of the calorifier in terms analogous to a storage cistern; for a heating element sized to generate hot water at a rate MN, the necessary hot water storage is given by XY, for the demand pattern shown. By varying the slope of MN, i.e., by simulating a different rate of generating hot water, the resulting storage requirements can be obtained. If this is done systematically, the relationship between rate of generation of hot water (and hence size of heating element)

Figure 5.3

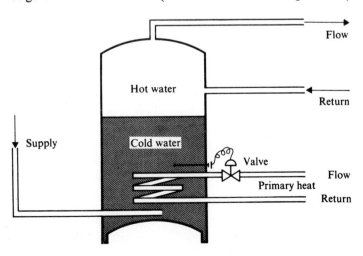

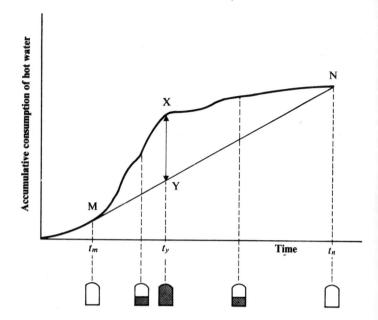

Figure 5.4

and storage (and hence calorifier size) can be produced, as shown in Figure 5.5.

All points on the graph in Figure 5.5 represent combinations of storage and rate of generation of hot water which will satisfy the given demand. The problem of selecting the most economic combination has still to be solved. Before this can be done however, the heat flow laws relevant to the calorifier must be considered. Heat flow from the heating element to the cold water in the calorifier will, as outlined in a previous chapter, depend on the surface areas and the nature of the heating conductor and, if the primary heat source is a fluid heat transfer medium, on its rate of flow through the conductor. In sizing the heating element to

Figure 5.5

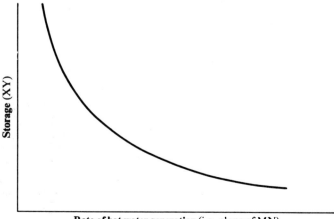

generate the required volume of hot water, account must be taken of the heat loss from the walls of the calorifier to the surrounding air and of the loss from the flow and return distribution pipework; as previously noted these losses can be reduced by insulation. When the rate of hot water generation has been translated into size of heating element, the costing exercise can begin.

The costs associated with the storage, all of which relate to volume, are: the cost of the vessel itself; the cost of the space it occupies; the cost of insulation.

The costs associated with the size of the heating element are: the cost of the element itself; the cost of the primary heat generating plant, if applicable, (e.g., boiler).

Where the costs are a mixture of capital and recurring costs, the equivalent annual or present worth should be used. The axes of Figure 5.5 can now be changed to cost units and lines of constant cost plotted (Figure 5.6). The point of tangency between the original curve and the minimum line of constant cost (C) gives the optimum (i.e., minimum cost) solution.

Now, in the argument that has been developed, the analysis was described in terms of the demand on a single day whereas it has been stated that demand will be variable from day to day. The daily variation can be dealt with by applying the line MN to each day in a sample period and plotting

Figure 5.6

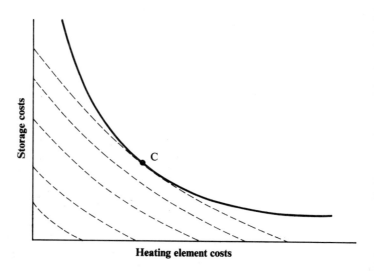

Heating element costs

the distribution of the resulting storage values XY. The actual storage to be supplied for any rate of hot water generation can then be determined by conducting a cost-benefit analysis in which the cost of storage is added to the costs consequent on a failure to satisfy the demand for hot water on a particular day, as outlined in Chapter 4.

In a large building complex, consideration can be given to the provision of several calorifiers, each serving a zone within the complex as opposed to the provision of a single, centrally located calorifier. The economic comparison between the centralized and decentralized systems should take account of:
(a) the cost of the primary distribution (which will be greater in the case of the decentralized system),
(b) the cost of the secondary distribution (which will be greater in the case of the centralized system), and
(c) the cost of the calorifier(s) (which will be greater in the case of the decentralized system).
The greater calorifier cost in the decentralized system is accounted for in the main by two factors: the multiplication of control apparatus and fittings; and the reduction in demand diversity, as shown by the equation on page 23.

Distribution
The problem of distribution of hot or cold water to outlets sited throughout a building can be seen as that of allocating the available pressure head most economically throughout the system while satisfying the pressure and flow requirements at each outlet. This can be represented, for a 'tree' distribution, in Figure 5.7, assuming the same pressure and flow are required at each outlet. The actual arrangement of the branches and the pressure levels chosen should be such that the total cost is minimized.

Figure 5.7

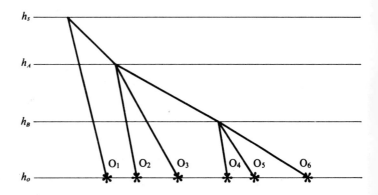

Analysis, as before, starts with data on demand; i.e., data on the utilization of each type of outlet. As has already been shown, the number of outlets in simultaneous use is likely to conform to a binomial distribution, i.e., if the probability of any one of the outlets O_4, O_5 and O_6 being in use is p, then the probability of all three being in simultaneous use is given by

$$_3C_3(p)^3(1-p)^{3-3} = (p)^3.$$

Since p is less than 1 in value, the more outlets which are considered together, the lower is the probability that all will be in simultaneous use. The decision as to how many should be catered for in the design is a cost-benefit one in which the costs of meeting the demand of, say, x in use simultaneously are summed with the costs consequent on failure to satisfy the demand at the remaining outlets, and a minimum total cost sought.

When the decision as to what proportion of the demand is to be satisfied is taken, the flow in each section of the distribution network is known. The procedure then is to set the intermediate levels of pressure head h_A, h_B arbitrarily and, knowing the length of each branch, compute the required diameter of each branch from the equation

$$\Delta h = F \frac{v^x}{d^y} \rho l$$

where Δh is the difference in pressure head (taking account of elevation) between the two ends of the branch under consideration. Knowing lengths and diameters, the cost of the pipework can be calculated. The arbitrary levels of pressure head can now be changed and the computation repeated to determine if the pipework cost can be reduced. By this iterative procedure, the optimum sizing of the network can be determined.

It should be noted that where a building comprises a set of replicated facilities (e.g., a hospital with, say, 20 similar wards) the diversity of water outlet use over time may have important implications for the optimum distribution strategy. Consider Figure 5.8 in which two distribution strategies are proposed for a multi-storey ward block. If the ward blocks are similar in layout, the first distribution will tend to collect similar outlets on the vertical rises, whereas the second distribution will tend to collect dissimilar outlets on the horizontal runs. Because ward activity is in part routine, outlets of a certain type in one ward are likely to be in use

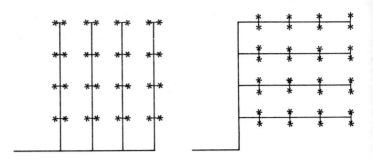

Figure 5.8

at the same time as the same type of outlet in all other wards. Thus the first of the two distribution networks has an inherent disadvantage. In certain cases this disadvantage may be compensated for by the fact that isolation of any pipe run during maintenance work is less disruptive.

It should be clear that for economy in distribution, areas of the building in which demands for hot and cold water are high, cooking areas, laundry areas, bathing areas, etc., should be sited near the supply point. If there are other reasons for siting them remotely from the supply point these should be economically justified. In any event, the siting of outlets should not be decided prior to consideration of the servicing implications.

The sizing of 'tree' distribution networks, although fairly complex in itself, is considerably simpler than the sizing of ring or grid distribution networks; this fact may be the reason why the advantages of pipework rings or grids are seldom made use of in practice. In essence, water drawn from an outlet sited on a ring or a grid may flow to the outlet by more than one route and therefore pipework diameters can be smaller. The sizing techniques, based on the pressure drop and volumetric flow relationships given in the section beginning on page 120 are admirably suited to the iterative processes of the electronic computer and will not be detailed here but the principle of economic optimiza-tion – trading off increases in pipework length with decreases in pipework diameter – is similar to what has already been covered in this section.

The flow and return system of distributing hot water from a calorifier is in fact a ring circuit. The purpose of the pump in this circuit is simply to keep 'live' hot water flowing round the building; the sizing of the pump will be determined by the losses incurred in achieving low velocity flow round the circuit. Heat loss from the distribution pipework can be reduced by insulation and by arranging for the pump to shut off at periods when demand is zero.

Change in requirements over time

Statistical techniques for the forecasting of future demands were introduced in Chapter 2; these, used in conjunction with a commonsense prediction of how requirements will alter in the future due to sociological change and technological innovation, can be the means of determining a design strategy which is robust, in economic terms, over the life of the building. One approach is to produce design schemes for various points in time and then to determine what characteristics the initial scheme should embody to facilitate the most economic transformation sequence from any one scheme to any other.

Two trends relating to the design of hot and cold water plant are worth mentioning: the general level of amenity, i.e., the number of water outlets readily accessible by users, is on the increase and the quantity of water used in a single operation of a fixture (e.g., a WC) is being reduced; this would seem to portend a greater rate of growth in instantaneous demand than in total demand. The major problem relates therefore, to the distribution network rather than to the calorifier and storage tanks. Now it has already been shown that, due to the binomial or Poisson nature of the utilization of outlets, diversity increases with the number of outlets served (Figure 5.9 gives the number of outlets, each with a probability of use of 0·5 which must be considered in simultaneous use to satisfy 95% of the demand). Obviously the addition of a certain number of outlets to a circuit which already serves a large number of outlets has less effect on pipe sizing than the proportional addition to a number of circuits each serving a small number of outlets. It follows that a distribution circuit which 'collects' a large number of outlets (and ring circuits tend to do this), although initially

Figure 5.9

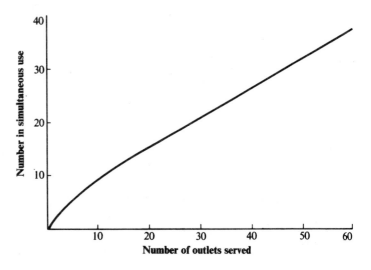

not the most economic solution, may be most economic over the life of the building.

Current design recommendations and regulations
The standard design guide for the sizing of hot and cold water supply and distribution plant is the *Guide to Current Practice*[1] produced by the Institution of Heating and Ventilating Engineers. Information contained in the *Guide* ranges from theoretical formulae, through the properties of materials to empirical plant sizes and much of this is of great value to the designer. It does not, in the author's opinion, obviate the need on the designer's part to conduct fundamental analysis of specific design problems in the manner outlined in the foregoing sections.

Regulations relating to the design and installation of hot and cold water plant are contained in the *Building Regulations*.[2] Other regulating codes, relating to the design and manufacture of hot and cold water plant are CP 342: Part 1: 1970 *Centralized Domestic Hot Water Supply. Individual dwellings*, CP 3 (1950) *Engineering and Utility Services*, and CP 310 (1950) *Water supply*, produced by the British Standards Institution.[3,4,5]

Electrical services

Electricity may be used in buildings for a wide variety of purposes: lighting; power for fixed equipment such as lift motors; power for portable equipment such as vacuum cleaners; cooking; space heating; transmitting information; and controlling other engineering services.

A typical system
In a large building it is usual to have a three-phase, four-wire supply (215 V phase voltage, 415 V line voltage) as shown in Figure 3.19; the four wires are made up of the three-phase wires (referred to as red, yellow and blue) and

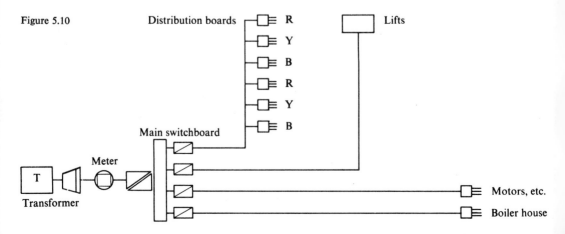

Figure 5.10

the neutral wire. Where the supply is obtained from the local electricity board, a meter is provided to record the consumption over a quarter, and, if applicable, the maximum demand within a given period. Immediately after the electricity board meter the supply passes through the main fused switch and into the main distribution board. From here, a number of sub-mains, independently fused and switched, distribute the supply to the final distribution boards sited at various locations throughout the building (Figure 5.10). Circuits from the final distribution board, independently fused and switched, may be two-wire single-phase, or if motors are supplied, three-wire three-phase. The degree of division and sub-division of the main supply is dependent on the degree of control which is desired over the isolation of specific demand points.

In certain building types in which a break in the electricity board supply would have serious consequences (e.g., a hospital) it is normal to make provision for the emergency supply of electricity to certain areas of the building. This may be done by starting up a diesel generator or, if the load is light, by switching over to a bank of batteries; where even a few seconds' break in supply is serious, it may be necessary to use batteries to meet the load while the diesel generator is running up to speed. The distribution of the emergency supply may be by means of the existing distribution boards and cables but more often a completely independent distribution system is provided to give cover not only for breaks in the electricity board supply but also for failure in the distribution network within the building.

Distribution
As with the hot and cold water pipework, the analysis of an electricity network starts with data on the demand, i.e., data on the utilization of electrical equipment and outlets. The distribution of simultaneity of use can be obtained from existing buildings, and, if as is likely, it conforms to a binomial distribution, the probability of any number of simultaneous uses obtained from the formula $_nC_r(p)^r(1-p)^{n-r}$. At any demand point there is a requirement for a certain current at a certain voltage, and the cables supplying the current must be sized accordingly. Cables are rated in terms of their current-carrying capacity and selection should be made in accordance with the expected current flow, with a check made that the voltage drop over the cable is not so large as to adversely affect the functioning of the apparatus being supplied.

95

To prevent damage to the cables and the fire hazard due to overheating consequent on too great a current flow, a fuseable link, or equivalent device is incorporated in the circuit. As with the cable, the fuse will be sized in relation to the predicted simultaneity of demand. The presence of the fusable link in the circuit means that the economic analysis used to obtain a minimum cost solution will be slightly different from that employed in the case of water pipe sizing; since all demands greater than the design demand will blow the fuse, the failure will be total rather than partial, and the costing of the consequences should take account of this.

Figure 5.10 shows a distribution system which basically comprises a vertical sub-main serving sub-circuits which run horizontally on each floor of the building; an alternative distribution strategy is a horizontal sub-main serving vertical sub-circuits. The factors which must be considered in determining the best distribution strategy are:
(a) the diversity of use between demand points, and
(b) the convenience of isolating certain groups of demand points.

In a multi-storey building with a large number of 'repeat' floors, the strategy illustrated in Figure 5.10 has advantages on both counts. While it is normal practice to arrange the main distribution in 'tree' form, it is becoming increasingly common to provide a single-phase 'ring' sub-circuit to serve socket outlets and certain fixed equipment in individual areas of the building (Figure 5.11); the advantages to be gained are analogous to those relating to the distribution of water.

For perfectly balanced three-phase loads such as motors, pumps, oil burners, a three-wire three-phase circuit is adequate. Where the load on each phase of a three-phase supply is likely to be different, a fourth wire, neutral, must be installed; to reduce the voltage drop over the neutral wire the loading should be allocated to the red, yellow and blue phases in such a way as to minimize the imbalance at any point in time. For a building with a large number of 'repeat' floors, it is common practice to 'rotate' the phases – red, yellow, blue, red, yellow, blue, etc., on each floor – as in Figure 5.10. In any event it is considered hazardous to arrange socket outlets on any one floor such that some are supplied from one phase and some from another phase. An error in wiring could result in a line voltage of 415 volts which could prove lethal.

It should be obvious, as it was with water distribution, that the more remote the electrical load is from the supply point the greater the distribution costs will be. There is thus a strong economic case for siting areas of the building which give rise to heavy electrical demand adjacent to the main distribution board.

Equipment for power factor correction

Equipment and appliances which operate on electro-magnetic principles – ac motors, transformers, fluorescent lighting, chokes, welding equipment, etc. – have a power factor less than unity (see pages 61 and 81). The most efficient method of correcting the power factor is to install capacitance either at each source of the reactive current or centrally. The financial return in terms of a reduced electricity bill for a capital investment in capacitance has already been covered in the section dealing with electricity tariffs (Chapter 4); the additional return for installing individual capacitance at the source of the reactive current can be evaluated by costing the reduction in switchgear and cable sizing throughout the distribution system.

Generating plant

Breaks in the supply of electricity from the local electricity board are not unknown and in certain building types consideration may be given to the provision of an alternative

Figure 5.11

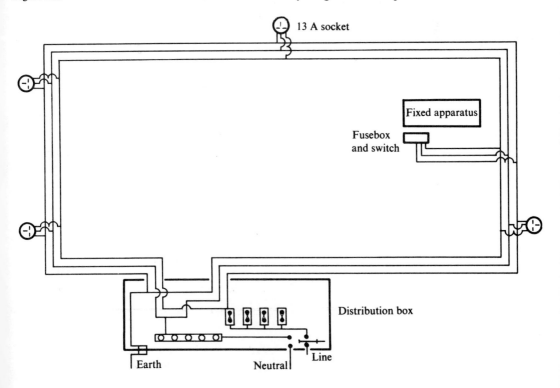

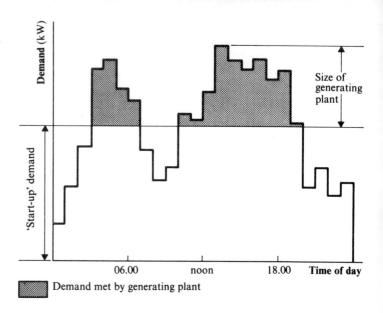

Figure 5.12

Demand met by generating plant

supply by generating electricity on site. For a building housing a commercial process, such as nylon spinning, the economic analysis relating to local generation may be straightforward; the variables which must be taken into account are:

(a) the expected frequency and duration of breaks in the electricity board supply,

(b) the capital and recurring cost of the generating plant (including depreciation, maintenance, space, etc.), and

(c) the cost consequences of failure in supply – lost production, wastage, etc.

In non-commercial building types such as a hospital, the consequences of a break in the electricity board supply may be extremely serious but not easily costed and the designer is presented with a difficult design decision. One way out of the problem is to seek an economic justification for the plant quite independent of its emergency function; if this can be established, the emergency function may be considered as a 'bonus'. Now, it has already been stated on page 79 that if electricity is bought from the board on a maximum demand tariff, the price of every unit consumed in a given period is positively related to the magnitude of the maximum demand occurring within that period; thus, the higher the maximum demand (measured over 30 minutes), the more *every* unit of electricity used costs the consumer. It follows that if the consumer is able to reduce the maximum rate of demand he may reduce his electricity bill dramatically.

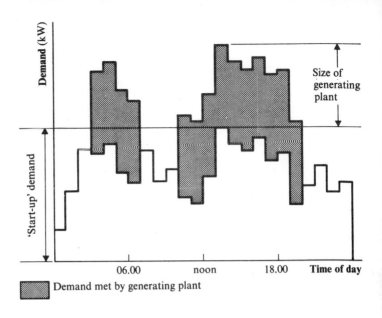

Figure 5.13

Basically, there are two ways in which stand-by generating plant could be used to reduce the maximum demand made on the electricity board supply:

(a) by operating the stand-by generator at varying loads, as illustrated in Figure 5.12, or

(b) by operating the stand-by generator at full load, as illustrated in Figure 5.13.

In both cases the generator is started manually or automatically when a certain magnitude of demand is reached. As the efficiency of diesel generating plant is greatly reduced at partial load, consideration in this section will be given only to plant operating automatically under full-load conditions.

To determine the optimum size of the generating plant, the following data are required:

(a) the pattern of total demand (monthly maxima and details of the half-hourly load in one summer week and one winter week are sufficient for the accuracy required),

(b) estimates of the cost-in-use (in present or annual worth) for different sizes of generator, and

(c) details of the relevant maximum demand tariff (expressed, preferably, in the form illustrated in Table 4.2).

The method of analysis is as follows:

(a) by subtracting each generator size from the annual maximum demand, the 'start-up' demand is obtained for each generator size.

99

(b) from the detailed data on the summer and winter weeks' demand, the number of hours during which each size of generator will run is computed for the summer and winter months; this can be done graphically as in Figure 5.13, taking account of the 'start-up' demand.

(c) the number of hours' running time for each generator size for each week in the year is obtained by considering proportions of the monthly maximum demand figures.

(d) the total number of units of electricity generated per month and annum can now be calculated together with reduction each month in the maximum demand; knowing the relevant tariff equations, e.g.,

$Mcost = £0·8375M$

$Ucost = £0·0040416U,$

the benefit, in terms of electricity bill reduction can be computed.

(e) knowing the cost-in-use of each size of generator (for the computed number of running hours) the cost investment per annum can be computed.

Figure 5.14 shows the results of an analysis of a hospital: the return is positive for generators of size between 75 kW and 180 kW and is optimum for a generator of size 140 kW. In the case of this particular hospital, a stand-by generator of size 50 kW had been installed but was not connected to the main distribution system within the building and therefore could not be used to reduce the peak load; clearly much greater emergency cover could have been given, the capital cost recovered and an annual 'profit' made, if a thorough analysis of the problem had been conducted at the design stage.

The use of stand-by generating plant for the reduction of maximum demand raises the question of whether or not the 'availability' of the plant in the event of a break in the electricity board supply, is reduced; in fact the serviceability

Figure 5.14

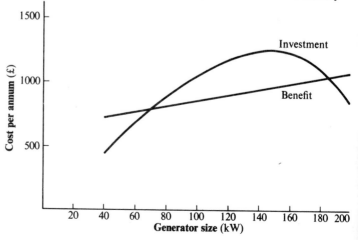

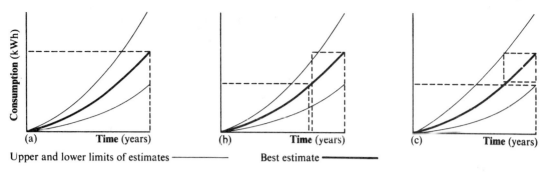

Upper and lower limits of estimates ———— Best estimate ━━━━

Figure 5.15

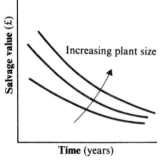

Figure 5.16

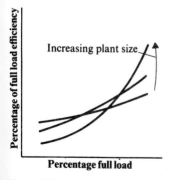

Figure 5.17

of diesel generating plant is increased by proper and regular running. The probability of a simultaneous failure of the board's supply and of the generating plant is thus reduced rather than increased.

Change in requirements over time
The dramatic rate of growth of demand for electricity in buildings is well known and may be accounted for by two main factors:
(a) the increasing number of types of fixed and movable electrical equipment available to the consumer as a means of automating his activities, and
(b) the continuing increase in environmental standards (such as illumination level) which make greater demands on the electrical service.

A trend towards increased consumption has implications for the electrical plant – generators, capacitors, etc., and for the distribution cables. With regard to plant, three main strategies may be compared economically:
(a) initial oversizing,
(b) replacement as necessary,
(c) incremental additions.

Determination of the optimum strategy will depend on the life span of the plant, the confidence with which consumption forecasting can be made for increments in time up to the life span of the plant, and the efficiency of operation of the plant at partial load. The three strategies, in simplified form which assumes the life of the plant is equal to the life of the building, are shown in Figure 5.15; the data typified by Figures 5.16 and 5.17, together with the capital and operating costs are sufficient for the comparative analysis to be made. It will be clear that strategies (b) and (c) in Figure 5.15 have an inherent advantage if the actual consumption turns out to be lower than the best estimate. In any event, the spatial implications of the alternative strategies must be considered.

The arguments put forward on pages 93–4 hold equally for the problem of how growth in consumption affects the cable network: the 'robustness' of a circuit with regard to increased load is positively correlated to the amount of load it is initially designed to meet. Even if it is economically advisable to replace the wiring in a building area once or more than once in its lifetime, the intervals between replacement may be increased by a disproportionately small increase in investment initially to ensure maximum demand diversity on each circuit. If re-wiring is the best strategy, the cost may again be reduced by provision initially of conduit and junction boxes which reduce the re-wiring labour.

Current design recommendations and regulations

The Institution of Electrical Engineers produces *Regulations for the Electrical Equipment of Buildings* (known as the IEE *Regulations*[6]) which contain reference to all appropriate British Standard Codes of Practice and Specifications. The IEE *Regulations* set out what is considered to be a suitable minimum standard of wiring but, while it would be folly to ignore them (since electricity boards consider a system which complies with the *Regulations* as 'safe' by definition) the author's intention in this section has been to encourage a more basic consideration of the electrical design problem than is afforded by reference solely to the *Regulations*.

Gas services

The use of gas in buildings, whether 'town' gas – a by-product of the production of coke – or natural gas, is mainly as a source of heat in cooking and space heating and as a source of fire for the incineration of waste materials. In laboratories, bunsen burners are widely used as a readily controllable heat source.

Figure 5.18

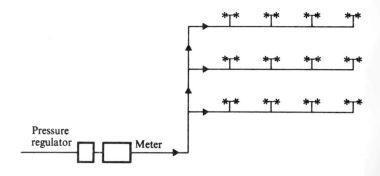

Pressure regulator   Meter

A typical system

Figure 5.18 shows a typical gas service distribution system. Gas, supplied at a pressure slightly above atmosphere from the local gas board is metered on entry to the building and is distributed to outlets throughout the building. The distribution system shown in the Figure is of 'tree' form but a ring circuit or grid are feasible alternatives.

Distribution

Design of the distribution network must be such that an adequate volumetric flow at the desired pressure can be obtained from the outlet points in use at any time. The first stage in the design task is a statistical calculation of the probability of simultaneous usage of the outlets, given the probability of use of any individual outlet. The calculation is analogous to that described for water outlets and employs the binomial expression

$$_nC_r(p)^r(1-p)^{n-r}.$$

Knowing the number in simultaneous use and the required flow at each, the flow in any branch of the distribution network is known. The problem is then one of allocating the available pressure head to each section of the network such that the piping costs are minimized. This can be solved, as in the case of water distribution, by setting an initial and arbitrary pressure drop in each section and calculating the resulting pipe diameter from the appropriate formula which, as seen on page 54, has the form

$$\text{pressure drop, } \Delta h = F\frac{v^x}{d^y}\rho l.$$

Economic optimization is achieved by iteratively modifying the arbitrary pressure levels and costing the pipework on each successive cycle.

The interaction between the spatial layout and the water and electricity distribution networks, which has been already discussed, has a parallel when the gas distribution system is being considered. 'Dis-economies' are encountered when demand points, particularly those where demand is high, are sited remotely from the supply point. Moreover, the initial cost of the network, and its potential to satisfy a growth in demand, will depend on the degree to which the network can efficiently 'collect' large numbers of outlets which have a high demand diversity.

Heating and air conditioning

The main purpose of heating and air conditioning services is to provide, in conjunction with the shelter afforded by the fabric, a controlled level of thermal environment in the building. While it is not within the scope of this text to deal with the criteria for thermal comfort, it is worth stating that it depends on:

(a) the temperature of the air surrounding the human body,
(b) the temperature of the adjacent surfaces,
(c) the relative humidity of the air, and
(d) the motion of the air.

A secondary, and in some building types very important, function of the air conditioning system is to increase the level of air hygiene by removing from the air dust particles, bacteria, gases and other matters of a noxious or unpleasant nature.

The study of heating and air conditioning systems is a complex one since the fabric and contents of the building are themselves an integral part of the system. A further difficulty is due to the fact that the rate of flow of heat through most media between points of different thermal 'potential', is, when compared to electricity or water, extremely slow; any analysis of a dynamic system must therefore take account of this thermal lag or inertia.

Typical systems

Figures 5.19(a) and 5.19(b) show, in very simple diagrammatic form, typical heating systems. In Figure 5.19(a) heat from a primary heat medium is given up to a secondary heat transfer medium (which may be any stable fluid, but is most commonly water or steam) in a heat exchanger. This medium is circulated (by pump or natural convection)

Figure 5.19 (a)

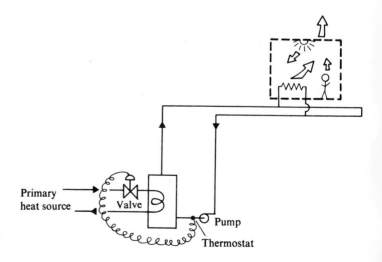

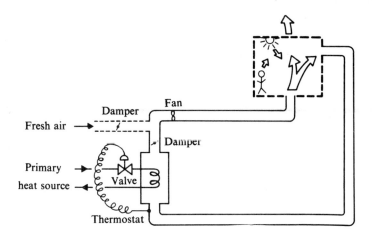

Fan

Damper

Fresh air →

Damper

Primary →

heat source ◄—

Valve

Thermostat

Figure 5.19 (b)

to various locations in the building where it passes through
another heat exchanger designed to maximize the rate of
heat transfer between the secondary heat transfer medium
and the surrounding air. Heat may also be added to the air
from the human occupants and from equipment such as
lighting fittings. The final heat transfer apparatus is the
building fabric itself; when the outside air temperature is
lower than the indoor temperature, heat will flow through the
fabric and through apertures in the fabric to be dissipated in
the environment at large.

In Figure 5.19(b) the main difference lies in the fact that the
secondary heat transfer medium is air and the space in the
occupied area of the building is an integral part of this
secondary circuit. The fan which moves the air round the
circuit may be sited in the flow or return side of the heat
exchanger, depending on whether a positive or negative
pressure in the living space, relative to the outside, is required. Control of the heat input to the secondary circuit
can, in both cases, be achieved by thermostatic control of the
primary heat source. Balance of the flows to different areas
of the building can be achieved by check valves in the case
of the water or steam circuit and by dampers in the case of
the air circuit.

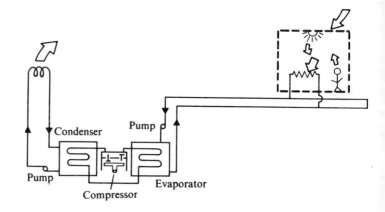

Figure 5.20 (a)

Typical cooling systems, represented diagrammatically in Figures 5.20(a) and 5.20(b), are analogous to the heating systems just described. In Figure 5.20(a) a compression refrigerator (as described on page 63) removes heat from the secondary heat transfer medium and rejects it to the atmosphere. The cooled medium is then circulated round the building to the appropriate locations. In Figure 5.20(b), the secondary heat transfer medium is air, and, as in Figure 5.19(b), the space to be cooled is an integral part of the secondary distribution system.

It is not uncommon for the same secondary distribution system to be used for both heating and cooling.

Dynamic heat balance
Design of heating and cooling systems starts with data on the extreme temperature variations and solar conditions, and on the internal sources of heat gain and loss; these data, taken in conjunction with the characteristics of the building fabric and orientation, are the basis for the sizing of the plant.

Figure 5.20 (b)

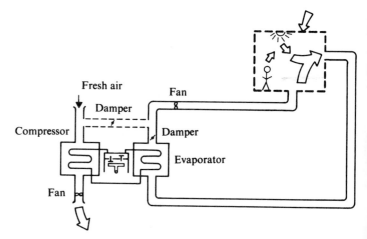

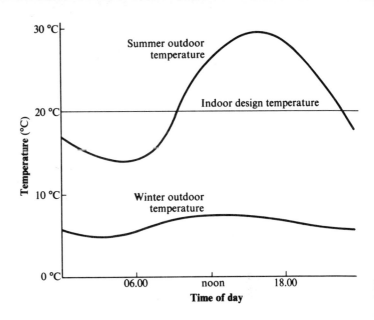

Figure 5.21

Figure 5.21 provides, as a starting point, a comparison of the external air temperatures on an extreme summer and winter day with what may be an acceptable internal temperature range.

Since the fabric of the building has a thermal mass and resistance, however, the internal temperature variations, assuming no heating or cooling system is in operation, will be out of phase with, and will be different in amplitude from, the external temperature conditions. Assuming a constant warm indoor temperature, the variation in heat losses

Figure 5.22

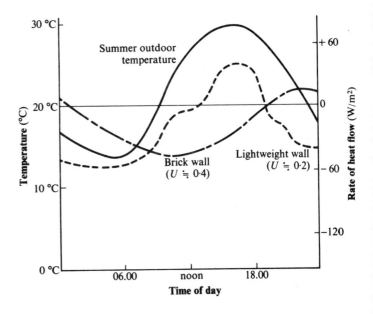

107

throughout a summer or winter day can be calculated from the external temperature conditions by applying the equation of the rate of heating or cooling and the equation of thermal transmittance for any type of building fabric (see page 47). Figure 5.22 compares the fabric heat flow with external temperature conditions for two types of building construction.

Solar heat gain through glazing depends, as established on page 49, mainly on the area of glazing and the orientation of the glazing. Values of solar heat gain throughout the year for a location in the British Isles are given in Figure 5.23, and Figure 5.24 gives the variation over a summer day.

Like solar gains, heat flow due to ventilation tends to be in phase with the variations in outdoor temperature; provided the amount of air flow due to window and door opening and due to cracks and gaps in the structure can be estimated, the heat flow can be calculated as shown on page 49.

Figure 5.23

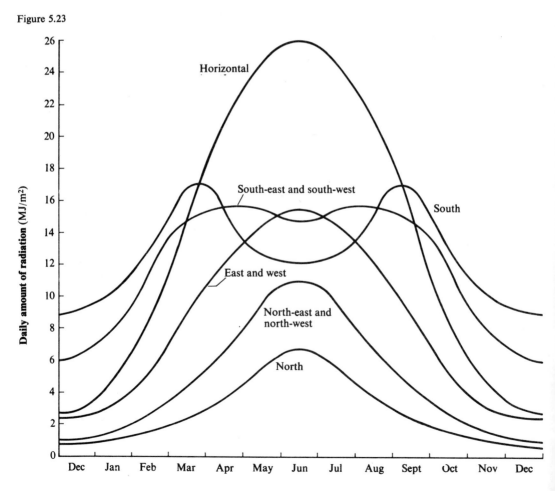

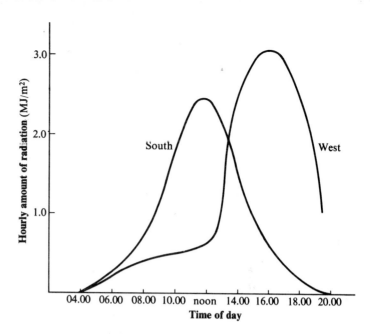

Figure 5.24

Internal heat gains, assuming a constant indoor temperature, can be fairly easily computed. The heat output of humans engaged in a variety of different activities has been tabulated and the output of equipment such as lighting fittings, is usually known. It is thus possible to produce a graph of the hourly variation, summer and winter, of internal heat gain.

By combining the hourly figures of heat flow, due to transmittance through the fabric, solar radiation, ventilation, human occupation and use of equipment, a picture of the loadings on summer and winter days can be produced. In proportion, the total daily gains and losses for typical days in each month can be plotted for the year as a whole; Figure 5.25 records these for an 800-pupil school.

Some thought must be given to the choice of the meteorological data employed in the analysis of the loadings. To identify extreme winter temperature conditions, a distribution of winter minima over a number of years may be plotted in a frequency distribution and, for a given probability, the extreme condition identified; the same procedure is appropriate to summer conditions. When a heavy structure is being investigated, however, the combination of several cold (or warm) days may be more relevant.

The purpose of the heating and cooling plant is to balance out the heat gains and losses and thus maintain the internal environment at a constant and desirable temperature. This may be done by the addition or removal of heat, or by

109

transferring heat from one section of the building where there are major gains to another section where there are major losses.

It should be clear from the foregoing that the nature of the construction of the building and its orientation are major variables in the optimum design of the heating and cooling systems. The penalty for confirming decisions regarding fabric and orientation prior to, or independent of, investigation of the thermal implications may be extremely high either in economic terms or in terms of performance.

Figure 5.25

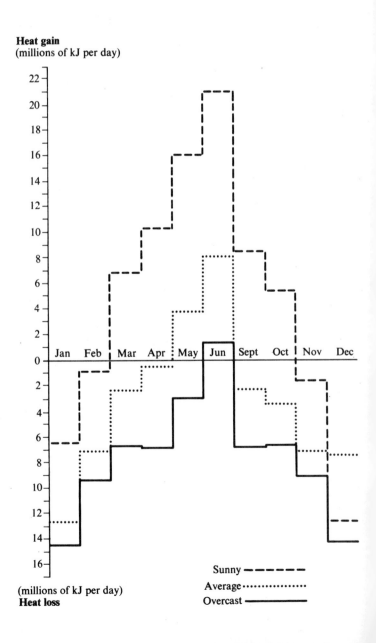

Heat gain
(millions of kJ per day)

(millions of kJ per day)
Heat loss

Sunny — — — — —
Average ················
Overcast ———————

Plant

Due to the stabilizing effect of the fabric and the contents of a building, the fluctuations on the loading of the heating and cooling plant are less rapid than on the plant, say, for generation of hot water. It is uncommon, therefore, to maintain a reservoir of the heat transfer medium, although the economics of storage could be investigated using a procedure similar to that on pages 87–90. Without storage, the calorifier in the heating system must be designed to exchange heat from the primary heat source to the transfer medium at a rate which is equal to the maximum rate of heat losses of the area of the building served plus any losses incurred in the distribution system; similarly, the refrigerator in the cooling system must be designed to exchange heat to the refrigerating medium from the transfer medium at a rate which is equal to the maximum rate of heat gain in the area of the building served plus any gains incurred in the distribution system. At periods of less than maximum loading, the total amount of heat transfer is reduced by thermostatic control, based on the return temperature of the transfer media, of the supply of heat in the case of the heating system, or of the operation of the compressor in the case of the cooling system.

The sizing of the surface of the heat exchange coils will depend, as stated on page 51, on the rates of flow of the primary and secondary media and on the nature of the material of the coils. In the case of the cooling plant, the maximum heat transfer rate will dictate the size of the compressor and of the waste heat exchanger.

Before leaving the discussion on plant it is worthwhile referring to pages 62–3 where the nature of thermodynamic exchange is discussed. There, the refrigerator was identified as a particular application of the heat pump; it follows that, by changing over the connections in the compressor refrigerator, heat could be 'pumped' from some external source (the air, a river, lake or the soil) into the building in winter. The potential exists, therefore, for using the same plant to heat and to cool the building.

In the case of the heat pump described on page 63, mechanical work is applied to the refrigerant fluid. An alternative type of heat pump cycle is one in which salt solution, by absorption of water vapour, promotes the evaporation of a reservoir of water, thus cooling it. The salt solution may be maintained at the correct concentration by driving off the excess water with heat, and the cycle completed by condensing this water vapour and returning it to the reservoir.

Thus, as in the domestic gas refrigerator, heat replaces mechanical work in the cycle. It follows that the primary heat source used in a heating system could also be used in a cooling system which utilizes the absorption heat pump cycle.

In summary, either a primary heat source or a source of mechanical energy may be used in both heating and cooling systems. The implications of this fact will be explored further in the following chapter.

Distribution media and systems
The 'heat energy capacity' of the distribution medium depends, as implied on page 51, on the specific (and latent) heat of the fluid, its temperature and its volumetric flow. Thus, to deliver the same amount of heating or cooling, the volumetric flow of a fluid with a low specific heat and a limit on temperature (because, as in the case of air, it is in direct contact with the occupants of the building), will be greater than the volumetric flow of high specific heat, high temperature media. If the distribution circuit is pressurized, circulation temperatures in excess of those at which the fluid normally changes state can be utilized.

The most common media are steam, high, medium or low pressure hot water, air and, more recently, organic fluids. The choice between them is a complex one but the principles of decision-making are similar in nature to those already developed in earlier sections, i.e., the economic comparison based on cost-in-use. The features of the distribution system of each of the media are different and each of the four will be dealt with in turn.

Steam heating
As heat is added to water there is an increase in its temperature and therefore it is sensible heat. When the temperature reaches boiling point (100 °C at atmospheric pressure), the temperature remains constant but the fluid changes state, from water to steam. The heat added during the change of state is the latent heat of evaporation. In comparison to the sensible heat of water at 100 °C, the latent heat of steam at the same temperature is very high, namely:
sensible heat of the water = 0·418 68 MJ/kg
latent heat of the steam = 2·256 22 MJ/kg.

Thus, if steam is circulated round a building and is caused to condense at specific points, the high latent heat contained in it will be given up.

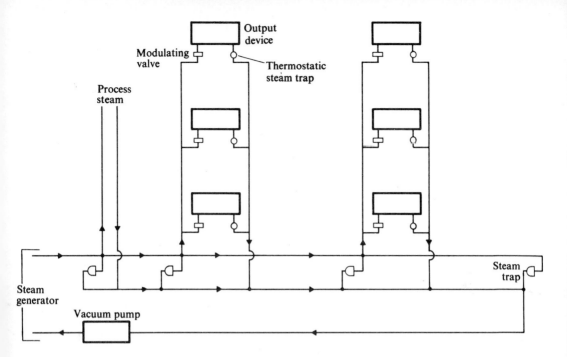

Figure 5.26

Figure 5.26 illustrates one configuration for a vacuum steam heating system. Steam at about 70 mN/m² is piped to convectors (or radiators or other heating apparatus) throughout the building. Control of the steam into each convector, and hence the heat emitted from it, is achieved by means of a modulating valve which may be adjusted manually. A pump sited at the low point of the circuit produces a vacuum in the condensate return pipework and thus draws water back from the convectors and returns it to the steam generator.

To avoid the live steam being drawn through the condensate pipework, the outlet from each convector is fitted with a thermostatically operated steam trap; the higher temperature of steam will keep the trap closed, whereas when condensate gathers in the convector, the lower water temperature will open the valve. Steam traps may be fitted at other points in the circuit where condensate is likely to gather, as shown in Figure 5.26.

A large variety of standard types of heater are available and the choice will depend on the nature of the space to be heated and the thermal environment desired. Convectors consist of a metal housing through which the steam pipes, possibly fitted with fins to increase the surface contact with the air, pass. The high temperature of the steam pipes causes air to be drawn in at the bottom of the housing and flow from a grill at the top; the flow of air through the convector can be

113

reduced by closing a damper and this affords some measure of control over heat output: convectors fitted with thermostatically controlled fans may be used where a high heat output is required.

For very high output, in an environment in which noise can be tolerated, 'unit heaters' may be used. In these, air at high velocity is blown by a fan past a bundle of finned steam coils in such a way that the warmed air is projected towards the desired location. As with fan convectors, the air being warmed may be drawn entirely from the space being heated (in 100% recirculation) or part may be drawn fresh from outside the building.

A third type of heater is the radiant panel in which the steam coils are normally welded to a steel plate which acts as a radiant surface. Due to the high surface temperature, radiators of this type have to be sited either at high level or in a location which prevents human contact with the panel.

Provided that the pipework system is so designed to deliver to each heater a quantity and quality of steam within known limits, the sizing of the heater becomes one of selection from a manufacturer's catalogue. Sizing of the distribution pipework, however, is a highly specialized job and only the main principles, which have a correlation to the design of the building as a whole, will be dealt with here.

The criteria for the sizing of the steam flow and condensate return pipework are quite different in so far as the fluid in each and the pressure in each are different. In both cases the laws of heat and fluid flow, in conjunction with the economic laws must be considered in relation to the configuration over time of the loading pattern throughout the building. The general strategy of distribution should, as in the case of hot and cold water distribution, take account of diversity in loading to ensure the most economic compromise between length of pipe run and pipe diameter is achieved. In buildings where, due to orientation or differences in occupancy, the heating loads in separate sections of the building are quite disparate, the distribution may be 'zoned' (see page 116 and Figure 5.28) with independent thermostatic control over each zone. For economy and ease of control over the heating in individual areas, extraneous emission of heat from the pipework can be reduced by insulation.

To promote comparison of different heat transfer media the advantages and disadvantages of a vacuum steam system are listed.

The advantages are:
(a) a high heat content per unit weight,
(b) rapid response rate due to the low thermal inertia of the medium.

The disadvantages are:
(a) the amount of ancillary equipment (steam traps, etc.) necessary to separate the steam from the condensate,
(b) the maintenance required by the ancillary equipment,
(c) the effect the lapses of maintenance have on the efficiency of operation of the ancillaries and hence on the system as a whole,
(d) the difficulty of designing efficiently to take account of the variation in performance over time of the ancillaries,
(e) the propensity towards corrosion in condensate lines.

Low, medium and high pressure hot water
Water at atmospheric pressure can be used as a heat transfer medium. While the simplicity of a low pressure hot water system gives it many advantages over a vacuum steam system, its main disadvantage, in large installations, is its low heat carrying capacity. To overcome this disadvantage, medium and high pressure hot water systems have been developed in which it is possible to circulate water at temperatures up to 177 °C.

Figure 5.27 diagrammatically represents a high pressure hot water system and illustrates one means of maintaining the system under pressure. The pressure vessel is filled partly with water and partly with gas or air supplied by either a compressor or a pressurized cylinder through a regulating valve. The water is circulated to convectors, radiators or

Figure 5.27

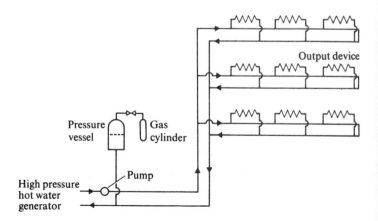

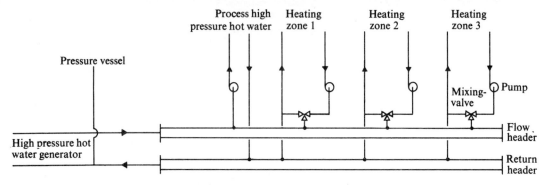

Figure 5.28

unit heaters throughout the building by means of flow and return pipework; the maximum flow through a heater can be set by means of a valve on the inlet side and variable control of flow up to the maximum can be achieved by means of a hand valve at the outlet.

In a low (atmospheric) pressure hot water system, the pressure cylinder would be replaced by a vent to atmosphere.

Figure 5.28 shows the pipework arrangement for a high pressure hot water system designed to serve three zones of a building each of which has different heat requirements. Temperature control in each zone is effected thermostatically or manually by the mixing valve which adjusts the amount of return water which is fed back into the flow.

As with steam, the types and ratings of space heaters – convector, radiator, unit heater – can be selected from manufacturers' catalogues knowing the nature of the space to be heated, the thermal environment desired, and the temperature and flow of the hot water being supplied.

The advantages of a high pressure hot water heating system are:
(a) the high heat content per unit volume,
(b) the ease of control of flow in individual sections of the network.
The disadvantages are:
(a) slow response rate due to the high thermal inertia of the medium,
(b) the high surface temperatures of the pipework,
(c) the need for a pressurizing system,
(d) the need for pipework, valves, etc., to withstand the operating pressure.

Chilled water cooling
Just as hot water can be used as a transfer medium for the heating of buildings, so chilled water can be used as a transfer medium for the cooling of buildings. Since a chilled

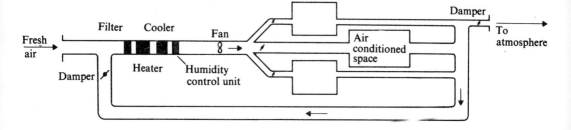

Figure 5.29

water system is used most often in conjunction with an air distribution system, however, it will be discussed at greater length under combined systems.

Air heating and cooling

As has already been stated, air may be used as a heat transfer medium for the heating and cooling of areas within a building. One of the advantages of an air distribution system is that control over the quality of the air – its cleanliness and its moisture content – can be effected as well as control over its temperature. Figure 5.29 illustrates a central air distribution system in which a mixture of fresh air and recirculated air is drawn through the filter, over a heating coil, cooling coil and humidity control unit and forced round a system of ducting to different locations in the building. Air from individual spaces may be exhausted to atmosphere (if pollution has become heavy) or recirculated by a system of return ducts to the central plant.

If the requirements for heating and cooling are quite different in different sections of the building, the distribution may be 'zoned' as in the case of high pressure hot water heating. Figure 5.30 shows the central plant serving three different zones: in effect, three separate air conditioning plants are employed. As an alternative to the system illustrated in Figure 5.30, a 'dual-duct' technique may be employed to satisfy different loading requirements throughout the building; in the dual-duct system, Figure 5.31, one duct carries warmed air, the other carries cooled air and mixing takes place in suitable proportions at each individual location.

Figure 5.30

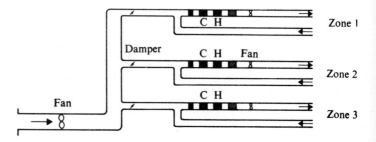

117

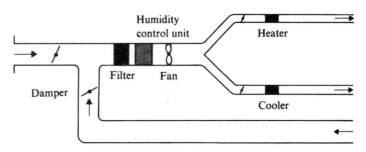

Figure 5.31

In all the systems illustrated, air temperatures and volumes can be controlled within certain limits. Control of air volumes in individual sections of the distribution network is by means of dampers which may be manually or thermostatically operated.

In a centralized air conditioning system there is no direct equivalent to the output devices, such as convectors, radiators and unit heaters, used in steam or high pressure hot water systems since the air itself issues into the conditioned space. There are, however, a variety of ways of introducing the conditioned air – by means of grilles, louvres or perforated ceiling panels. The choice of type of input device and the location of input and output devices will depend on the nature of the space to be conditioned and the conditions desired within it; as such, they are outwith the scope of this book.

In the sizing of the distribution ductwork, account may have to be taken of the interconnections (openings, doorways) between contiguous air conditioned spaces, since the space itself is an integral part of the distribution network. Due to the fact that warm air rises, a 'stack' effect in a multi-storey building may be quite marked and should be accounted for in design calculations.

The main advantages and disadvantages which differentiate a centralized air conditioning system from other heating and cooling systems are listed to promote comparison.

The advantages are:
(a) the facility for improving the 'quality' of the air in terms of hygiene and humidity,
(b) rapid response rate due to the low thermal inertia of the medium.
The disadvantages are:
(a) the low heat content per unit volume,
(b) the ease with which noise may be transmitted through the medium from a source to other parts of the building.

Organic fluid heating

Although they have been used for the distribution of heat used for industrial processes for some time, organic fluids as transfer media have only recently been used in space heating systems. The ideal organic heat transfer medium is one with a high specific heat which is also stable at high temperatures; thus, even at atmospheric pressure, the medium may be circulated at temperatures up to 320 °C, giving a very high heat capacity per unit volume. In principle, the design of an organic fluid heating system is similar to that of a high pressure hot water system; while the main advantage lies in the fact that high temperatures are attainable without a pressurized circuit, special care must be taken in the design of the pipework to avoid bursts which could, in the space heating context, have disastrous consequences.

Combined systems

Combined systems are defined, for the purpose of this test, as systems employing two or more distribution media. One example is an extension of the system represented in Figure 5.30; separate conditioning plant is sited within or adjacent to each room and is supplied from a distribution of fresh air and hot or chilled water. Figure 5.32 represents such a system in which both hot and chilled water are supplied, giving complete local heat control by the regulation of flows in the hot and cold pipe. More commonly, one pipe-work circuit serves the air conditioning unit through which hot or chilled water flows; the water supply can be changed over from summer to winter or zoned, within any season, such that some areas are supplied with hot water, others with chilled water.

Figure 5.32

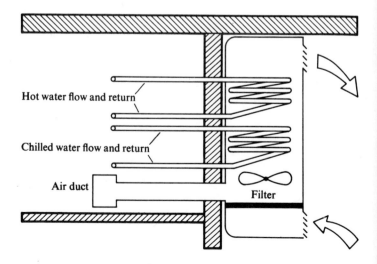

Hot water flow and return

Chilled water flow and return

Air duct

Filter

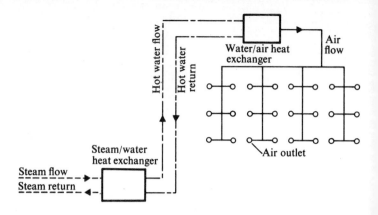

Figure 5.33

A number of variations on the system is possible:
(a) a certain degree of pre-heating or pre-cooling may be carried out centrally on the fresh air,
(b) the fan in the local unit can be dispensed with by introducing the fresh air through nozzles, thus inducing a certain amount of recirculatory flow,
(c) if the fan is retained, the fresh air supply ductwork can be dispensed with by introducing fresh air, filtered but otherwise untreated, locally at each unit.

It is worthwhile drawing a distinction between combined systems which operate in parallel, as does the system in Figure 5.32, with the exchange between the two media taking place locally, and combined systems which operate serially, such as that shown in Figure 5.33. In this system, three media – steam, hot water and air, for example – are serially linked by heat exchange apparatus. A decision to employ a number of media in this way may be occasioned by the suitability of each of the media to the characteristics of individual sections of the distribution network. In any event, such a system is only viable where a temperature differential exists between the media, thus,

$$T_{steam} > T_{hot\ water} > T_{air}.$$

Design of distribution networks
The sizing of heating networks economically is a very difficult business. The standard works on the subject deal with the problem by means of empirical equations and data tables, but, in accordance with the policy set out in the opening chapter of this book, the principles only will be dealt with here. The example used is relevant to the sizing

120

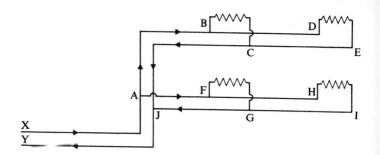

Figure 5.34

of a high pressure hot water network; application to other media may be determined by analogy.

Figure 5.34 illustrates a simple high pressure hot water distribution and Figure 5.35 is the corresponding network representation. Now, the heat flow from any segment of the network, say, BC, is given by

$$\dot{Q}_{BC} = (\dot{V}_3 - \dot{V}_4)\Delta T_{BC} c'$$

where $\dot{V}_3 - \dot{V}_4$ = flow along BC

T_{BC} = temperature drop along BC

c' = specific heat of water (expressed per unit volume).

Thus, $\Delta T_{BC} = \dfrac{\dot{Q}_{BC}}{\dot{V}_3 - \dot{V}_4} \times \dfrac{1}{c'}$.

But, according to the laws of heat flow networks, the algebraic sum of the temperature differences round any closed loop in the circuit is zero; thus in BDEC,

$$\Delta T_{BD} + \Delta T_{DE} + \Delta T_{EC} + \Delta T_{BC} = 0$$

i.e.,

$$\left(\frac{1}{c'} \times \frac{\dot{Q}_{BD}}{\dot{V}_4}\right) + \left(\frac{1}{c'} \times \frac{\dot{Q}_{DE}}{\dot{V}_4}\right) + \left(\frac{1}{c'} \times \frac{\dot{Q}_{EC}}{\dot{V}_4}\right) + \left(\frac{1}{c'} \times \frac{\dot{Q}_{BC}}{\dot{V}_3 - \dot{V}_4}\right) = 0$$

i.e., $$\frac{\dot{Q}_{BD}}{\dot{V}_4} + \frac{\dot{Q}_{DE}}{\dot{V}_4} + \frac{\dot{Q}_{EC}}{\dot{V}_4} + \frac{\dot{Q}_{BC}}{\dot{V}_3 - \dot{V}_4} = 0$$

Figure 5.35

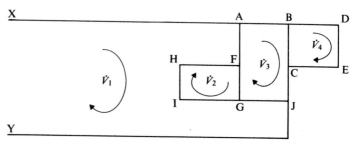

121

Analogous equations can be set down for each of the circuits; for the circuit XAFHIGJY, the equation will have the term $c'\Delta T_{XY}$ on the right-hand side, where ΔT_{XY} is the temperature difference between the flow and return.

The next stage in the analysis is to insert values for the heat loss in each segment of the network. For a segment such as BC, the heat loss will be the required output of the heating device; for a segment such as BD, the heat loss should be set at a value which is a reasonable estimate of the pipework heat loss, or at zero. If an arbitrary (but reasonable) value is now given to the temperature difference between flow and return (ΔT_{XY}), four equations with four unknowns ($\dot{V}_1$, $\dot{V}_2$, $\dot{V}_3$, $\dot{V}_4$) are available for solving. The method of solution is by iterative approximation (for which the digital computer is ideally suited).

Having computed $\dot{V}_1$, $\dot{V}_2$, $\dot{V}_3$, $\dot{V}_4$ (on the basis of an arbitrary value of heat loss from the pipework segments and an arbitrary temperature difference between the flow and return), the next task is to determine the pipe sizes which will carry these flows. Since it is known that the algebraic sum of the pressure drops round any circuit is zero, it can be stated, for circuit XABDECJY, that

$$\Delta h_{XY} = \Delta h'_{XA} l_{XA} + \Delta h'_{AB} l_{AB} + \Delta h'_{BD} l_{BD} + \Delta h'_{DE} l_{DE}$$
$$+ \Delta h'_{EC} l_{EC} + \Delta h'_{CJ} l_{CJ} + \Delta h'_{JY} l_{JY}$$

where $\Delta h'_{XA}$, etc., is the pressure drop per unit length of pipe-run.

Now, assuming the pressure drop per unit length is uniform throughout this longest circuit, then,

$$\Delta h_{XY} = \Delta h'(l_{XA} + l_{AB} + l_{BD} + l_{DE} + l_{BC} + l_{CJ} + l_{JY})$$

i.e., $$\Delta h' = \frac{\Delta h_{XY}}{l_{XA} + l_{AB} + l_{BD} + l_{DE} + l_{EC} + l_{CJ} + l_{JY}}$$

and $$\Delta h^x = \frac{\dot{V}}{Kd^y}$$ for any section of the circuit.

Thus, if an arbitrary value is given to Δh_{XY}, then, knowing the length of any section of its circuit XABDECJY, its diameter may be calculated. The same process can now be applied to each smaller circuit in turn.

It will be remembered that, for the calculation of flow rates, assumptions were made regarding the heat loss from the pipework segments. It is now possible to go back and adjust these assumptions in the light of the diameters just computed, or, rather, their nearest commercially available equivalents. This may result, on recomputation, in different flow rates which in turn will give rise to different diameters. The technique is thus one of successive reiteration until two

Figure 5.36

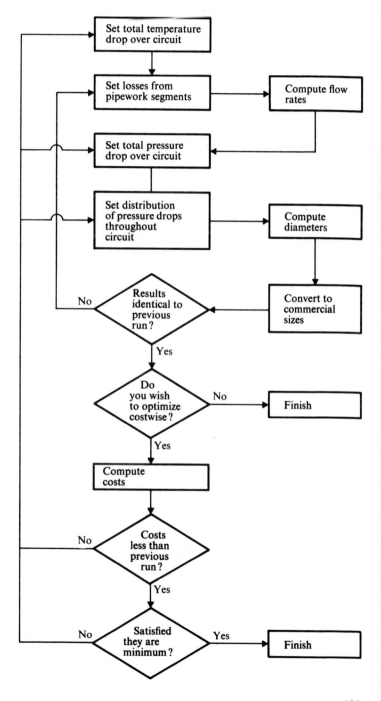

123

consecutive runs produce convergence on a set of identical results.

The outcome of the process thus far is a solution which is technologically feasible but which may not be optimum economically. The search for the economic optimum involves investigation of the effects of changing the assumptions regarding the total temperatue drop over the circuit, the total pressure drop over the circuit and the distribution of pressure drops round the circuit, but it will be obvious that the work involved, even with the help of a computer, is considerable; Figure 5.36 outlines the sequence of operations.

The computation of costs for a high pressure hot water network or for any other heating/cooling system should include the capital cost of the pipework (or ductwork), the capital cost of joints, fittings etc., the capital cost of insulation, the capital cost of the space taken up by the network (together with rates, taxes, etc.), the capital cost of the primary heat source and heat exchangers, the capital and running costs of the pumping apparatus, the capital cost of the output devices, the labour cost for installation, maintenance, supervision, the fuel costs (including the losses from the system), and the cost of the heat transfer medium, if applicable.

The costing exercise is only realistic, however, if the system under consideration is totally independent of other engineering services and of other aspects of the building design. Pages 127–8 in this chapter deal with the interaction of the heating/cooling systems with the construction, layout and orientation of the building and Chapter 6 attempts to take an overall view of the total interaction.

Direct heating and cooling by electricity
On page 58 it was shown that when an electrical current is passed through a resistance, the temperature of the resistance rises and heat is emitted from it. This phenomenon is the basis of systems which, as opposed to utilizing secondary or tertiary heat transfer media, use electricity directly for space heating.

Radiant electric heaters can be of the type which radiate heat directly from the exposed resistance, or element, or they can be of the panel type with the element in close proximity to a large ceramic or metal radiating surface. In convector heaters, the element is enclosed in a casing and air passes over it either by natural convection alone or assisted by a fan; high velocity fans can be used in unit heaters similar to those described on page 114 where it is desired to project the current of warm air some distance.

Now, it has already been shown on page 58 that the heat output from an element is inversely proportional to its resistance and hence directly proportional to the diameter divided by the length; it can also be stated that the temperature rise in the resistance is inversely proportional to its surface area. The implication of these relationships is as follows: for any supply voltage a given heat output can be obtained either by a low temperature element (which will be relatively long and have a relatively large cross-sectional area) or by a high temperature element (which will be relatively short and have a relatively small cross-sectional area). This choice of element temperature within a distribution system is a feature of direct electrical heating systems not shared by systems utilizing secondary flow media.

The fact that electricity can be purchased more cheaply from the supply authority during certain restricted hours has led to the development of systems in which heat is supplied to a reservoir during off-peak hours. Most commonly the reservoir is a mass of fireclay blocks or of water, contained in a steel cabinet, which is sited within the space to be heated; either the heat output is uncontrolled, via radiation and natural convection – in which case the efficiency of the insulation should be such that the heat output is 'paced' over the heating period, or the output can be controlled by thermostatic operation of a fan – in which case the thermal resistance of the cabinet should be high. The greater the specific heat of the storage medium, the greater will be the heat storage capacity of the reservoir per unit weight.

An alternative to employing a purpose-built reservoir, is to employ the building fabric itself as a heat store. This is done most commonly by embedding the appropriate length of low temperature element in the floor screeding. The first task in the consideration of underfloor electrical heating is to compare the configuration of heat losses in the space to be heated with the configuration of heat output from the system (Figure 5.37) to ensure that a satisfactory balance is struck during the hours of occupancy of the space.

Before leaving the subject of electrical heat output devices, it is worth mentioning the recent development of a conductive paint. Applied to a wall, with the electrical supply connected via two conductors, one running the length of the wall at floor level, the other running the length of the wall at

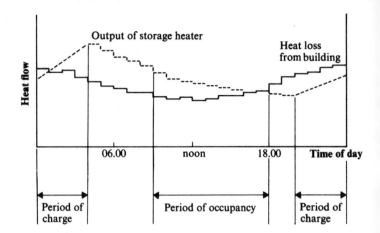

Figure 5.37

Output of storage heater

Heat loss from building

Heat flow

06.00   noon   18.00   **Time of day**

Period of charge

Period of occupancy

Period of charge

ceiling level, low temperature heat is emitted into the room. Little can be said at this time about the characteristics of such a system other than that it appears to offer great potential for the integration of the heating system into the interior design of individual spaces.

Cooling by electricity is normally carried out by what is known as a through-the-wall, air-to-air conditioning unit. Figure 5.38 illustrates such a unit in which electricity is used to drive the compressor and the fans. The volume of fresh air intake can be controlled by means of a damper sited in a duct through the outside wall. If a heating coil is also fitted, the unit can be used for cooling in summer and heating in winter. Where noise production must be kept to a minimum, an absorption type refrigerator may be used.

Figure 5.38

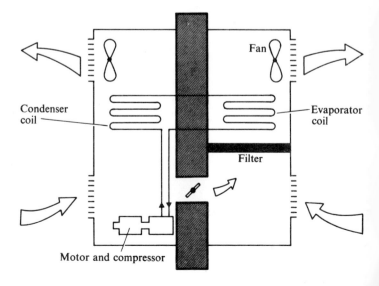

Fan

Condenser coil

Evaporator coil

Filter

Motor and compressor

Distribution

Electrical distribution has been covered in an earlier section and little needs to be added here. If heating is to be by off-peak electricity, supplied from the local authority grid, a separate distribution system, centrally controlled by a time switch, will be required.

Thermoelectric heating and cooling

On page 64 the principle of thermoelectric conversion was stated. With recent advances in semi-conductor materials, the use of bi-metal circuits for heating and cooling in buildings has become feasible. The most direct way of utilizing the characteristics of the circuit is to site one junction on the inside surface of an external wall, the other on the outside surface. In summer, direct current flows through the circuit with the consequence that the inside junction takes in heat; in winter, the flow of current is reversed and the inside junction gives out heat.

Direct heating and cooling by gas

The combustion of town or natural gas may be used as a means of heating in radiant fires, convectors or unit heaters. The main difference between direct heating by gas and direct heating by electricity lies in the fact that provision should be made in a gas system to exhaust the gaseous products of combustion to the atmosphere. Cooling by gas is possible using a through-the-wall, air-to-air conditioning unit fitted with an absorption type refrigeration cycle. Distribution of the gas throughout the building has already been dealt with in principle on page 103.

Interaction between heating and cooling systems and the building

As stated on page 104 there is major interaction between the heating/cooling system and other aspects of the building design. These interactions will be dealt with under three headings: construction, orientation and layout.

Construction

The materials used in construction have considerable effect on the nature of the heating and cooling load. The thermal transmittance of the materials affects the total flow of heat through the building fabric and, thus, the magnitude of the heating and cooling load. The mass and the specific heat of the materials affect the thermal capacity of the fabric and, thus, the magnitude and phasing of the heating and cooling load.

Orientation

As seen in Figure 5.23, the heat gain through glass is dependent on the orientation of the glazed area. Thus, the magnitude of the heating and cooling load will depend on general orientation of the building and on the provision of windows on each vertical surface.

Layout

The implications of the layout of the building, in so far as it affects the external surface area and the relative location of the spaces which require to be heated and cooled, are considerable. In the first place, since rate of heat transfer is directly proportional to surface area, the heating load in a building of given volume will be greater in a 'dispersed' layout than in a 'compact' layout; on the other hand, if the building is so compact that excess internal heat gains cannot be dissipated, the cooling load will be considerable. In the second place, it will be clear that the costs associated with the distribution network will correlate to the distance of the spaces to be heated and cooled from the location of the primary heat (or cooling) source; a layout which allows grouping of the load points as close as possible to their 'centre of gravity' will obviously be most efficient. The relative location of load points also has implications for the facility with which a zoning control policy can be implemented.

Change in requirements over time

The problem of a change in heating and cooling requirements over time would seem to be, fortunately, less acute than in the case of demand for hot water and electricity, and it is difficult to foresee a heating and cooling system with proper control facility which is properly maintained becoming inadequate, other than by physical degradation of its constituent parts. If there is a possibility that the building will 'grow' during its lifetime, however, the designer must investigate the alternative strategies of providing additional and separate plant to meet the loads in the 'growth' when the time comes, or of initially providing redundant space and/or plant sufficient for the extension of the existing system.

Current design recommendations and regulations

The process of sizing a heating or cooling distribution network from first principles, as exemplified in the section which begins on page 120, is a lengthy and skilled operation which requires the most up-to-date computational aids. While it is in keeping with the aims of this book to deal with the basic principles which constitute good design, it must also be said that a host of more expedient and pragmatic methods of sizing, which are not considered to contravene 'good practice' are available to the designer in texts devoted specially to this topic and in the *Guide* published by the Institution of Heating and Ventilating Engineers.[1] The *Guide* provides a mass of data on climatic conditions, transmittance co-efficients, flow characteristics of pipes and ducts, properties of fluids, criteria for comfort and statutory regulations which are invaluable to the designer of heating and cooling systems.

The *Building Regulations*[2] deal with the regulations pertaining to the design and installation of heating apparatus.

6 Total systems

In Chapter 5 the most common engineering services – hot and cold water, electricity, gas, heating and cooling – were dealt with as individual sub-systems. In this chapter, the attempt will be made to consider the services in a building, or in a group of buildings, as an integrated whole.

Energy exchange
As a starting point, a re-statement of the interchangeability of energy forms will be considered. Figure 6.1 states the exchanges which are practical within the present level of technology and the following sub-sections outline the current exchange techniques.

Figure 6.1

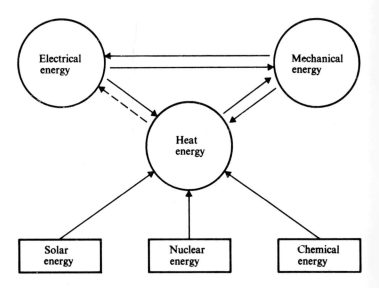

Solar energy to heat energy
Solar energy is converted to heat and light when the rays of the sun strike the earth; by arranging suitable apparatus, the heat may be collected and stored within the structure of the building itself or in a fluid heat transfer medium. As stated on page 39, the solar energy concentration is of the order of 1 kW/m² and clearly in a country such as the UK the collection area must be very large if the limited periods of sunshine are to be utilized effectively.

Nuclear energy to heat energy

Heat, at approximately 8×10^4 GJ/kg, is produced when nuclear fission takes place. The design of the reactor in which the fission is controlled is such that this method of heat production is feasible only on a very large scale.

Chemical energy to heat energy

The oxidation of the fossil fuels – coal, oil, natural gas – is exothermal in nature. The amount of heat given out in the chemical reaction ranges between 40 and 130 MJ/kg. By burning fossil fuels in a boiler, the heat output can be transferred to a fluid transfer medium for distribution to any desired location.

Heat energy to mechanical energy

As stated on page 62 there are several devices for the conversion of heat energy into mechanical energy – the internal combustion engine, the gas turbine, the steam engine and the pure air engine. It is important to re-state that the efficiency of the conversion approaches only 40% at best and heat must be rejected in the process.

Mechanical energy to heat energy

The heat pump or refrigerator which may be driven by a reciprocating or rotary engine converts mechanical energy into heat energy by 'pumping' low grade heat from one location to high grade heat at another. As stated on page 111 the direction of the pumping can be changed so that heat may be pumped into the building in winter and out of the building in summer.

Mechanical energy to electrical energy

When a generator is driven by a reciprocating engine or turbine, electrical energy is produced at efficiencies approaching 100%.

Electrical energy to mechanical energy

The electric motor is a device for converting electrical energy into mechanical energy. The exchange can be achieved at efficiencies approaching 100%.

Electrical energy to heat energy

The most common method of converting electrical energy to heat energy is by passing a current through a resistance which is situated in a fluid transfer medium; alternatively, the current can be passed through the transfer medium itself, as in the electrode boiler. A quite different principle is that of the bi-metal circuit, described on page 64, in which a direct current causes heat to be given out at one junction of the

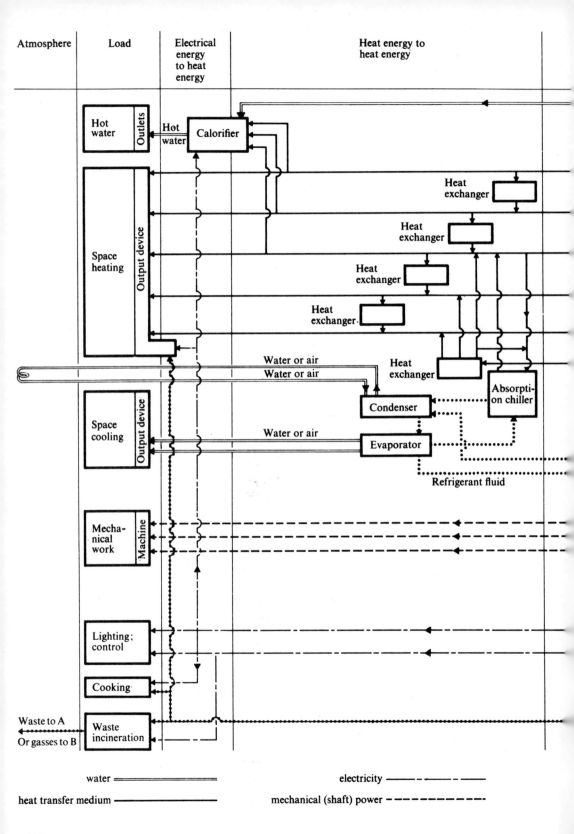

Atmosphere	Load	Electrical energy to heat energy	Heat energy to heat energy

Hot water — Outlets

Hot water — Calorifier

Space heating — Output device

Heat exchanger

Heat exchanger

Heat exchanger

Heat exchanger

Heat exchanger

Water or air
Water or air

Space cooling — Output device

Condenser

Water or air

Evaporator

Absorption chiller

Refrigerant fluid

Mechanical work — Machine

Lighting; control

Cooking

Waste to A
Or gasses to B — Waste incineration

water ══════════
heat transfer medium ─────────

electricity ─·─·─·─
mechanical (shaft) power ─ ─ ─ ─ ─

132

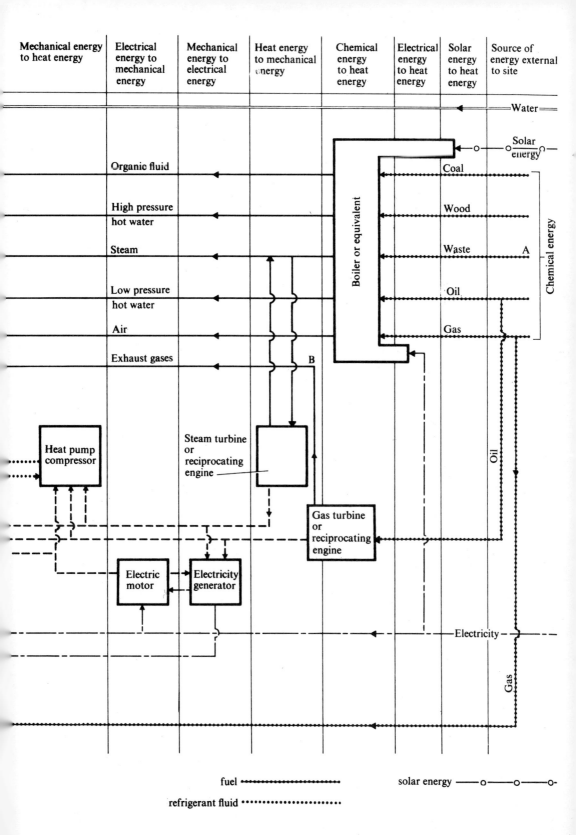

Mechanical energy to heat energy	Electrical energy to mechanical energy	Mechanical energy to electrical energy	Heat energy to mechanical energy	Chemical energy to heat energy	Electrical energy to heat energy	Solar energy to heat energy	Source of energy external to site

Water

Solar energy

Organic fluid

Coal

High pressure hot water

Wood

Steam

Waste   A

Low pressure hot water

Oil

Air

Gas

Exhaust gases

B

Boiler or equivalent

Chemical energy

Heat pump compressor

Steam turbine or reciprocating engine

Gas turbine or reciprocating engine

Oil

Electric motor

Electricity generator

Electricity

Gas

fuel ●●●●●●●●●●●●●●●●   solar energy ──o────o────o─

refrigerant fluid •••••••••••••••••••

133

circuit and taken in at the other. The conversion of electrical energy to other energy forms is achieved with very high efficiency whereas the conversion of heat energy to other energy forms has an associated 'wastage'; it follows that electrical energy should not, needlessly, be 'degraded' to heat energy.

Heat energy to electrical energy
The bi-metal circuit mentioned in the previous paragraph (and on page 64) can be used to convert heat energy to electrical energy. If heat is added to one junction and removed from the other junction, a direct current is set up in the circuit.

Figure 6.2 on pp. 132–3

From the foregoing it is clear that there is considerable scope for on-site conversion from one energy form to another and the designer must decide which basic forms are to be purchased and which are to be generated on site. Figure 6.2 summarizes the large number of alternative ways in which the engineering services loads may be met; as with the sub-systems, the choice of 'routes' taken in the system will depend on:
(a) the demand configuration,
(b) the relevant physical laws, and
(c) the costs.

Demand

Figure 6.3 represents the hypothetic hourly loadings in a building with respect to:
(a) heating load (in winter),
(b) cooling load (in summer),
(c) the hot water load,
(d) the mechanical load (lifts, motors, conveyors, etc.),
(e) the electrical load (lighting, etc.).

The loading levels are expressed relevant to a point immediately before the output device (i.e., radiator, unit heater, outlet, machine, fluorescent lamp, etc.) and are measured in power units (watts). The heating and cooling loads are drawn up assuming a given thermal response of the building fabric; as discussed on pages 127–8, different assumptions regarding mass, fenestration, plan shape and orientation would result in a heating load profile different in magnitude and shape from that shown. The magnitude and shape of the heating load profile may also be changed if the heat transfer medium meeting the load is storable. The effect of storage on the maximum primary heat source load for hot water has already been dealt with when discussing calorifiers (pages 87–90). Thus, the loading profiles in Figure 6.3 may be

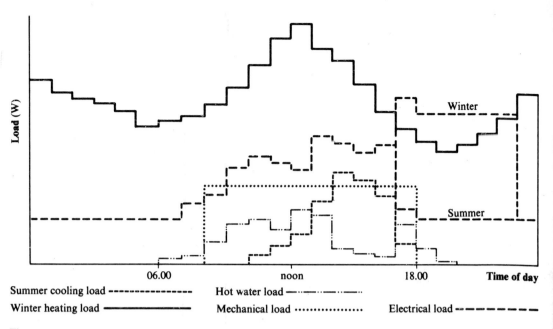

Load (W)

06.00　　　　　　noon　　　　　18.00　　Time of day

Winter

Summer

Summer cooling load ------------------　　　Hot water load —··—·—··—··　　Electrical load —— —— —— ——

Winter heating load ————————　　Mechanical load ················　　Electrical load

Figure 6.3

taken as a starting point, bearing in mind that the heating, cooling and hot water load profiles may, depending on other design variables, be different in configuration.

Alternative systems

A number of the alternative 'routes' in Figure 6.2 will now be explored in some detail in such a way that will promote comparison, and hence choice, between them.

Variant A

Consider Figure 6.4, gas (or oil) purchased from a supplier provides the fuel for a generator; the shaft rotation of the turbine is used to drive an electric generator, the output from which goes in part to meet the electrical load and in part to drive an electric motor which becomes the source of mechanical power. Now, as stated on page 131, in the process of converting heat energy to mechanical energy (which is part of the function performed by the gas turbine), heat is rejected. This heat, carried by the exhaust gases can be fed into a heat exchanger and used to generate steam which in turn provides the heat for a low pressure hot water heating system, an absorption chiller cooling system and a storage calorifier hot water system. The gas load is met by piping gas directly to the demand points.

A host of variations of this main theme is possible: where the mechanical load is sited close to the gas turbine, the load can be coupled directly to the turbine; alternatively steam can be piped to the location of the mechanical load and a steam turbine used as motive power; the electric

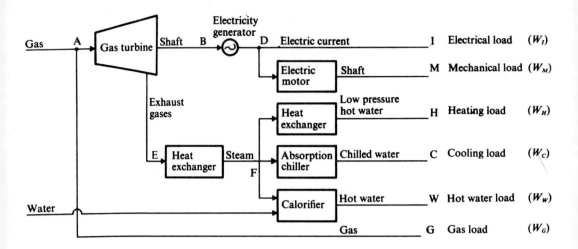

Figure 6.4

generator, as opposed to meeting the entire electrical load, can be used for peak-lopping only, as described on pages 97–101.

A system such as that proposed in Figure 6.4 must be checked for 'energy feasibility', i.e., are the disparate loads sufficiently balanced and complementary to allow efficient functioning of the system? This can be done by working back from the maximum individual loads, making allowance at each stage for the efficiency of the distribution system and the plant. The starting point is to pick off, from a loading analysis such as that given in Figure 6.3, the maximum heating load ($W_{H, max}$), the maximum cooling load ($W_{C, max}$), the maximum hot water load ($W_{W, max}$), the maximum mechanical load ($W_{M, max}$), and the maximum electrical load ($W_{I, max}$). The maxima for heating, cooling, hot water and mechanical work give rise to the sizing of the steam/water heat exchanger (P_{FH}), the absorption cooler (P_{FC}) and the hot water calorifier (P_{FW}); the maximum for mechanical work gives rise to the sizing of the electric motor (P_{DM}). Knowing the sizing of the individual items of plant, their efficiency, η, for any level of load can be obtained from manufacturers' literature.

Now, considering the loading conditions at time t, the loading at F ($W_{F,t}$) is given by

$$W_{F,t} = \frac{W_{H,t}}{\eta_{FH,t}} + \frac{W_{W,t}}{\eta_{FW,t}} \quad \left(= \frac{W_{C,t}}{\eta_{FC,t}} + \frac{W_{W,t}}{\eta_{FW,t}} \text{ in summer} \right)$$

where $\eta_{FH,t}$ is the efficiency of the plant and distribution system between F and H at time t, etc.

Similarly, the loading at D is given by

$$W_{D,t} = \frac{W_{M,t}}{\eta_{DM,t}} + \frac{W_{I,t}}{\eta_{DI,t}}.$$

Now, the size of plant and distribution system BD (P_{BD}) and EF (P_{EF}) can be obtained from $W_{D,\,max}$ and $W_{F,\,max}$; hence, from manufacturers' catalogues the efficiency characteristics, η_{BD} and η_{EF} can be obtained. Thus,

$$W_{B,t} = \frac{W_{D,t}}{\eta_{BD,t}} = \left(\frac{W_{M,t}}{\eta_{DM,t}} + \frac{W_{I,t}}{\eta_{DI,t}}\right) \times \frac{1}{\eta_{BD,t}}$$

and

$$W_{E,t} = \frac{W_{F,t}}{\eta_{EF,t}} = \left(\frac{W_{H,i}}{\eta_{FH,t}} + \frac{W_{W,t}}{\eta_{FW,t}}\right) \times \frac{1}{\eta_{EF,t}}.$$

The working of the gas turbine is such that the rate of output of heat in the form of exhaust gases increases and decreases in proportion to the rate of electricity generation. Thus: unless (a) the loads W_B and W_E are constant throughout the day (which is unlikely since that condition would depend on $\frac{W_M}{\eta_{DM}}$ and $\frac{W_I}{\eta_{DI}}$ being exactly complementary to each other *and* on $\frac{W_H}{\eta_{FH}}$ and $\frac{W_W}{\eta_{FW}}$ being exactly complementary to each other); or (b) the loads W_B and W_E vary in proportion to each other throughout the day (a more likely condition), then some heat output from the gas turbine will have to be wasted. Certain steps can be taken to promote conditions (a) and (b): as already mentioned, the space heating and cooling load is a function of building design and the loading configuration can be radically altered by considering alternative construction and layout solutions; it has also been mentioned that the hot water loading can be altered by using a calorifier with large storage capacity; and additional plant can be used to 'bridge' between separate branches of Figure 6.4 – e.g., the addition of a steam turbine would allow the mechanical load to be transferred back and forth between the 'branches' to adjust the cumulative loadings.

It should be noted that where a heated medium is stored, the analysis is rather more subtle. If a large hot water storage calorifier is employed to effect maximum shift in the load pattern, the demand, W_W, should be analysed as

137

described on pages 87–90 so that the relationship between the lowest feasible heating rate ($W_{W, \text{average}}$) and storage can be obtained. Knowing this, the efficiency of the calorifier is obtainable and the loading at F given as:

$$W_F = \frac{W_{H,t}}{\eta_{FH,t}} + \frac{W_{W, \text{average}}}{\eta_{FW,t}}.$$

Variant B

Figure 6.5 illustrates a system in which oil (or any other fossil fuel), purchased from a supplier, is burnt in a steam-raising boiler. The generated steam is used to drive a steam turbine which in turn drives an electricity generator. As with the gas turbine, the steam turbine rejects heat in operation and this can be used, as in variant A, for space heating, space cooling and hot water generation. The mechanical load is met by electric motors supplied from the generator. The gas load is met by piping gas directly to the demand points.

Again there is a host of minor variations possible: the mechanical load may be met directly from the steam turbine shaft or from a separate steam turbine, located near the mechanical load and taking steam directly from the boiler; the generator can meet part only of the electrical load as opposed to the full load.

Variant C

The main difference between this variant (Figure 6.6) and variant B is that the steam turbine is used to drive a compressor for the cooling system and the electrical load is met by purchasing electricity (on-peak and/or off-peak) from the local authority. The mechanical load is met by electric motors. Exhaust steam from the turbine is used for hot water heating, and space heating uses steam direct from the boilers.

Such a system is applicable to a situation where cooling is required throughout the year, perhaps in the central core of a deep building. An interesting variation would be to use a second compressor to operate a heat pump for space heating; the heat could be pumped from a nearby river or lake and supplemented by the waste heat from the cooling cycle.

Variant D

The main energy form purchased in this scheme (Figure 6.7) is electricity. The off-peak supply is connected to an electrode heater (in which the water, acting as a high resistance conductor, is raised in temperature); the high pressure hot

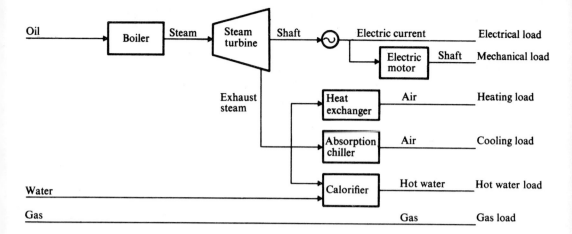

Figure 6.5

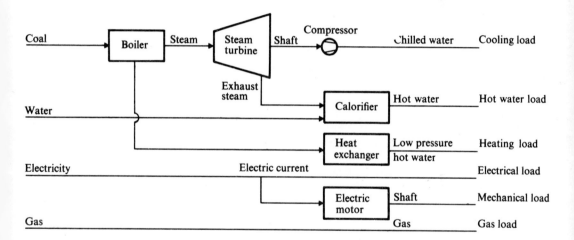

Figure 6.6

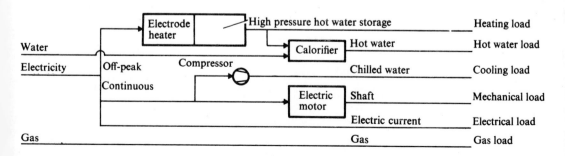

Figure 6.7

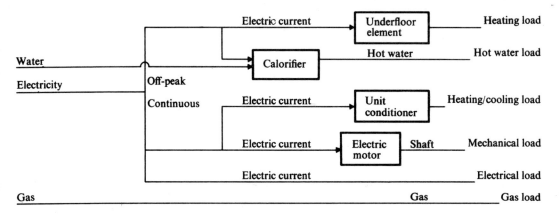

Figure 6.8

water generated is stored in a large cylinder from which
circulation round the building takes place. The hot water
demand is met from a calorifier supplied with heat from the
high pressure hot water circuit. The continuous electrical
supply drives a compressor for space cooling and electric
motors for mechanical power.

Variant E
Figure 6.8 illustrates a system in which the heating load is
met partially by under-floor elements supplied by off-peak
electricity, which also is used as the heat source in the hot
water calorifier. The remainder of the heating load, and the
summer cooling load, is met by unit air conditioners supplied
by electricity on the normal tariff. The electrical load and
the mechanical load are both met from the continuous
electric supply.

Other variants
Figures 6.4 to 6.8 illustrate but a few of the possible system
variants; from Figure 6.2 many more can be formulated.

Figure 6.9

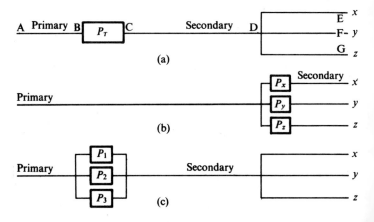

System design

Prior to an economic comparison being made between system variants, certain design factors have to be taken into account to ensure that the subsequent comparison is between the optimum configuration of each variant.

Consider Figure 6.9 in which three alternative ways of meeting the variable demands x, y and z are illustrated; in each case, plant, P, is required to convert the primary energy medium to a secondary energy medium. Two main (inter-related) design factors are to be considered: which plant configuration, P_T, $P_x P_y P_z$, or $P_1 P_2 P_3$ is optimum; and what proportionate lengths of primary and secondary distribution are optimum? It is assumed in the following argument that there is no storage element in the plant.

Since the demands x, y and z are variable, their maxima are unlikely to occur simultaneously, i.e., there is a diversity of demand. Thus,

$$\max(x+y+z)<(x_{max}+y_{max}+z_{max}),$$

thus,

$$P_T < P_x + P_y + P_z.$$

This inequality is a statement of the 'economy of scale' associated with meeting a number of demands from a single source. Where the diversity of demand between x, y and z is not high, however, but none the less each demand (and hence the total demand) is extremely variable, the economic advantage of scheme (a) over scheme (b) in capital cost terms may be more than offset in running cost terms due to the fact that the percentage full load on P_T, and hence its efficiency, will be less than on P_x, P_y and P_z.

Consider now scheme (c):

$$(P_1+P_2+P_3) = P_T$$
i.e., $(P_1+P_2+P_3) < (P_x+P_y+P_z).$

Thus the 'economy of scale' is preserved, and, due to the fact that any single element or any combination of two or three can be operated to match the total load, the operating efficiency will be relatively high. The choice of the relative sizing of P_1, P_2 and P_3 will relate to the configuration over time of the total demand, but it is interesting to note that if the sizing is chosen in the ratio $1 : 2 : 4$, it is possible to meet, at full operating efficiency, seven equal increments of load up to full load.

With regard to the distribution, something of the same logic applies. Consider scheme (a): the sizing of the three segments DE, DF and DG, will relate to x_{max}, y_{max} and z_{max}, whereas the sizing of segment BC will relate to $\max(x+y+z)$. Now, as before,

$$\max(x+y+z) < (x_{max}+y_{max}+z_{max})$$

thus there is advantage in retaining a common secondary distribution line as far as possible before a split is made. This is particularly true in pipes, where cost is more or less proportional to circumference, and hence to diameter, whereas carrying capacity is proportional to cross-sectional area, and hence to the square on the diameter; i.e., bigger pipes are proportionately cheaper than a number of smaller pipes, for the same loading.

The optimum location of the plant P_T along AD will relate to the cost of the primary distribution per unit length, c_{prim}, and the cost of the secondary distribution per unit length c_{sec}, taking account, if possible, of losses from both. Thus the location is defined by the expression

$$\min(c_{prim}\, l_{prim} + c_{sec}\, l_{sec}).$$

Cost comparisons

For consideration of the costs of any particular scheme it is appropriate to return to pages 135–8 and Figure 6.4. To simplify the analysis, it will be assumed that capital costs are directly proportional to plant and distribution network sizes. To recapitulate:
size of calorifier and distribution

$$= \frac{W_{W,\,max}}{\eta_{FW,\,max}} \quad \text{i.e., cost} = \frac{c_{FW} \times W_{W,\,max}}{\eta_{FW,\,max}} = C_{FW}$$

size of low pressure hot water heat exchanger and distribution

$$= \frac{W_{H,\,max}}{\eta_{FH,\,max}} \quad \text{i.e., cost} = \frac{c_{FH} \times W_{H,\,max}}{\eta_{FH,\,max}} = C_{FH}$$

size of steam heat exchanger and distribution

$$= \frac{W_{F,\,max}}{\eta_{EF,\,max}} \quad \text{i.e., cost} = \frac{c_{EF} \times W_{F,\,max}}{\eta_{EF,\,max}} = C_{EF}$$

etc.,

where c = capital cost of plant and distribution per unit of power,
C = capital cost of plant and distribution.

Similarly,

size of electric motor and distribution

$$= \frac{W_{M,\,max}}{\eta_{DM,\,max}} \quad \text{i.e., cost} = \frac{c_{DM} \times W_{M,\,max}}{\eta_{DM,\,max}} = C_{DM}$$

size of electrical load and distribution

$$= \frac{W_{I,\,max}}{\eta_{DI,\,max}} \quad \text{i.e., cost} = \frac{c_{DI} \times W_{I,\,max}}{\eta_{DI,\,max}} = C_{DI}$$

size of electric generator and distribution

$$= \frac{W_{D,\,max}}{\eta_{BD,\,max}} \quad \text{i.e., cost} = \frac{c_{BD} \times W_{D,\,max}}{\eta_{DI,\,max}} = C_{BD}.$$

Now, assuming the gas turbine is sized to meet the electricity generating load,

size of gas turbine and shaft connection

$$= \frac{W_{B,\,max}}{\eta_{AB,\,max}} \quad \text{i.e., cost} = \frac{c_{AB} \times W_{B,\,max}}{\eta_{AB,\,max}} = C_{AB}.$$

Thus, the total capital cost of the system shown in Figure 6.4 is

$$C_{capital} = C_{FW} + C_{FH} + C_{EF} + C_{DM} + C_{DI} + C_{BD} + C_{AB}.$$

The total amount of fuel consumed, in heat units per day, by the gas turbine is

$$\int_{t=1}^{t=24} \frac{W_{B,t}}{\eta_{AB}}.$$

Therefore, the fuel cost per annum is given as

$$c \left\{ \int_{1\,year} \left(\frac{W_{B,t}}{\eta_{AB,t}} + \frac{W_{G,t}}{\eta_{AG,t}} \right) \right\}$$

where c = cost of gas per unit of heat.

Thus, the present worth of fuel costs over the life of the building for the system shown in Figure 6.4, is given by

$$C_{\text{fuel}} = c \times \left(\frac{C_P}{C_A}\right) \times \left\{ \int_{1 \text{ year}} \left(\frac{W_{B,t}}{\eta_{AB,t}} + \frac{W_{G,t}}{\eta_{AG,t}}\right) \right\}$$

where $\left(\dfrac{C_P}{C_A}\right)$ is the appropriate interest factor (see Table 4.1).

The total cost of the system shown in Figure 6.4 (excluding water costs) is thus

$$C_{\text{total}} = C_{\text{capital}} + C_{\text{fuel}}.$$

The costing process just described is applicable, at a greater or lesser degree of detail, to any of the alternative systems and should be carried out if a true comparison between them is to be effected. Some rather coarse assumptions were made in the foregoing in the interests of descriptive clarity; a more thorough analysis would work not in unit capital costs but with the true cost functions for both plant and distribution networks. The assumption of unit fuel cost is also misleading; the fuel cost will of course depend on the tariff structure, as shown on pages 76–82.

Scale of operation

It will have become clear from the preceding chapters and the preceding section that a major factor in the design of engineering services is the scale of supply and distribution. Consider the simplified situation illustrated in Figure 6.10, in which the centre represents a point of supply and the crosses represent demand points. The relationship between the number of demand points and the length of the distribution network, taking each 'ring' of demand points in turn from the centre is:

Figure 6.10

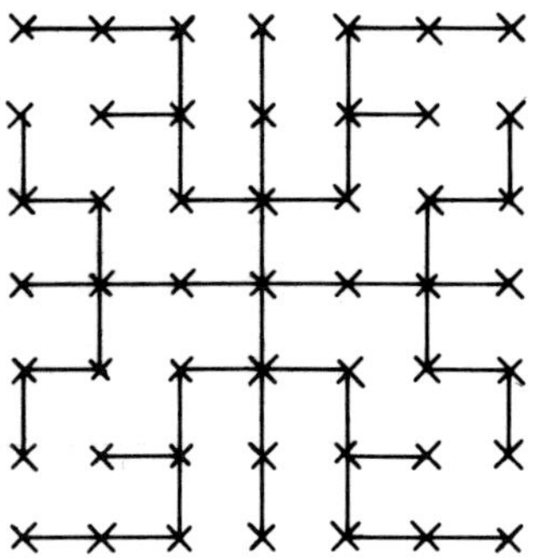

points served (A)	length of circuit (B)	A/B
8	8	1
24	24	1
48	48	1

i.e., the length of the circuit increases linearly with the number of points supplied. (Readers may care to try other branching distribution strategies; by adopting an inefficient strategy the ratio $\dfrac{A}{B}$ forms a series which, in the limit, is unity.)

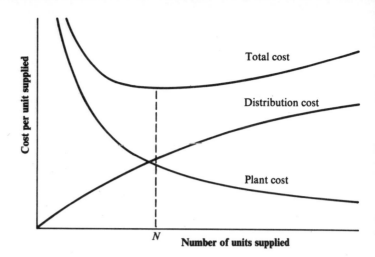

Figure 6.11

Now, due to the fact that there is a diversity of demand with respect to time between the demand points, coupled with the fact that large supply plant is proportionately cheaper than small supply plant, the unit cost of supply plant will decrease with the number of demand points supplied, as shown in Figure 6.11. On the other hand, since the length of distribution per demand point served does not decrease, whereas the diameter of some sections of it *increases*, the unit cost of the distribution will tend to increase with the number of demand points supplied (Figure 6.11).

Care should be taken in the interpretation of this last statement: it says, 'the greater the number of demand points served, the greater will be the distribution cost per demand point'. This in no way contradicts the argument developed in Chapter 5 which says, in effect, 'the more demand points which can be supplied by a single branch in a distribution network, the cheaper will be the distribution cost'.

If the plant costs and distribution costs are summed, as in Figure 6.11, a minimum is discerned. The number of demand points (N) corresponding to this minimum defines the optimum scale of operation. If it is required to supply $2N$ demand points, two separate (or better still, two interconnected) systems should be provided.

Now, it would be a fortunate thing indeed if the optimum number of demand points were of the same order of magnitude as the number of demand points in any given building, i.e., if the single building represented the optimum scale of operation for engineering services. Somehow, however, this is unlikely; otherwise the existence of central electricity

145

generating stations and central gas producing stations would be a nonsense.

If the optimum scale of operation is at the macro end of the scale, as the existence of the nationalized central generating stations seems to imply, the question of why is it worth considering economic on-site generation of these services is raised. The answer is simple: the central authorities, having no responsibility for the total provision of energy, wastefully discard energy in forms other than that which they are required to market. Thus, the choice which must be made by the unfortunate building designer is between:

(a) on-site generation at an inefficient scale of operation, or
(b) purchase of energy at a cost which reflects the inefficiency of its generation.

District schemes

When a large-scale development is being planned, the opportunity exists for investigation of efficient district schemes which will meet a number of the energy requirements from plant sited centrally. Figure 6.12 illustrates one possible configuration. Electricity is generated throughout the year and heat is supplied in the winter, cooling in the summer. In winter, hot water is generated on the consumers' premises using the high pressure hot water supplied from the central plant; in summer, when the electrical load is less, hot water can be generated on the consumers' premises with

Figure 6.12

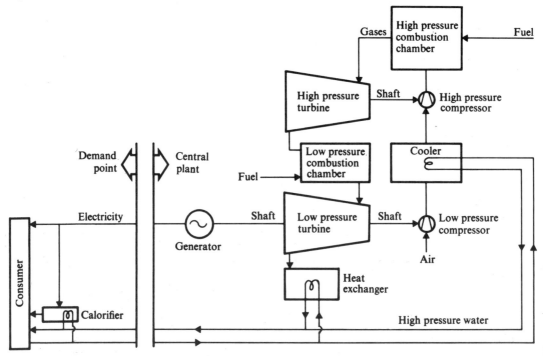

electricity. The consumption of electricity is metered in the normal way and consumption of heat energy may be metered by a device which integrates the product of flow and temperature difference over time.

At the beginning of Chapter 3, figures were quoted for the production of waste material in the UK. It has been estimated that the refuse collected from an urban area is sufficient to provide one-third of the heat requirements of the area, and it is therefore sensible to investigate the economics of using refuse as a supplement to the more conventional fuels.

Where the scale of operation being considered is relatively large, consideration can be given to the utilization of a nuclear reactor for heat generation. There are special problems associated with nuclear energy generation – the disposal of radioactive waste and the restrictions on proximity of the reactor to habitations – which should be settled at the outset by expert consultation.

The delineation of the district supplied, the characteristics of the load patterns of the different types of consumers and the potential for growth in the district, will all influence the nature of the central plant and its location within the district. The 'centre of gravity' of load at any point in time can be computed as shown in Figure 6.13. The 'centre of gravity' of the load at time t is at the origin when

$$W_{1,t}y_1 + W_{2,t}y_2 + W_{3,t}y_3 = W_{4,t}y_4 + W_{5,t}y_5 + W_{6,t}y_6$$

and

$$W_{1,t}x_1 + W_{2,t}x_2 + W_{6,t}x_6 = W_{3,t}x_3 + W_{4,t}x_4 + W_{5,t}x_5.$$

Figure 6.13

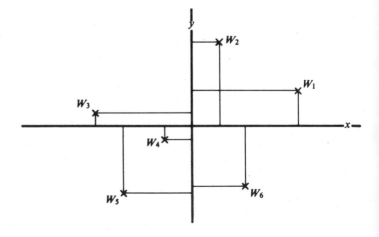

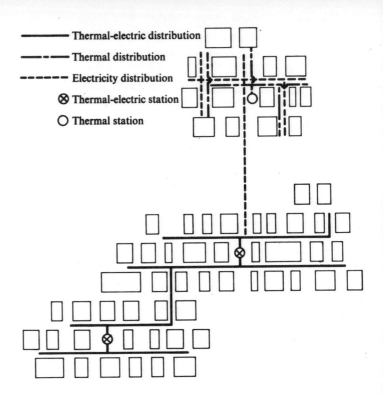

Figure 6.14

It is worthwhile determining the centre of gravity of the load at one or two points in time when the demand configuration is essentially different and selecting a location for the central plant by compromise between them. Proposed growth points of demand can be incorporated in the analysis to determine what influence they may have on the choice of location.

Figure 6.14 illustrates a system in which two interconnected thermal-electric stations meet the thermal and electrical load in a large section of the development, and the electrical load in a smaller section of the development. The thermal load in the smaller section is met from a purely thermal station equipped with fuel burning boilers. The choice of alternative district systems must depend, as it did with alternative on-site systems, on analysis of the nature of the demand load and the relative economics of supply and distribution. If it is possible to delineate districts such that in each there is a high concentration of consumers between which a high demand diversity exists, the chances of efficient system design and operation are increased.

The argument put forward on page 141 and Figure 6.9, for on-site plant comprising a number of discrete but interconnected elements, holds equally for plant in district systems.

It is common practice, where maximum (winter) load and minimum (summer) load are in the ratio of 2 : 1 and the total load is equivalent to five units, to provide three turbines (or three boilers) in the ratio 2 : 2 : 1. This strategy allows any one of the three turbines (or boilers) to be shut down for regular maintenance in the summer.

In Figure 6.11, the analysis of optimum scale of operation was based primarily on the grounds of plant and distribution costs. There are certain other, less tangible, factors to be taken into account which weigh in favour of a macro-scale solution. These are:
(a) the increased effectiveness of control over atmospheric pollution in a large central plant system,
(b) the decrease in road usage by oil tankers and coal trucks,
(c) the ability to monitor and record large samples of demand data for future design calculations, and
(d) the opportunity to employ high quality personnel for the effective real-time control of the system and for research and development work.

In summary, it must be stressed that:
(a) no service within a building should be considered in isolation from the other services,
(b) the interaction between the services in a building and the other aspects of the building system (construction, materials, orientation, plan layout) must be studied from the earliest possible stage in design, and
(c) study of the energy requirements of the built environment as a whole is properly within the responsibility of the architect/planner.

7 Implications for the future

Professional practice and education

In Chapter 1, two points were made which are worth re-stating:
(a) there is a high degree of interaction between the services system and other systems in the building, and
(b) the cost-in-use investment in the services system represents a very significant proportion of the total investment.

In subsequent chapters, some indication was given of the theories and methodologies appropriate to engineering services design studies. It is now appropriate to examine the systems of professional practice and education to determine whether or not the existing structures make it possible to tackle the problem of services system design in a manner which the importance of the topic justifies.

Up to this point in time, architectural undergraduate curricula have tended to deal very sketchily with engineering services: bye-laws and regulations were covered and standard systems provided for superimposition onto spatial solutions which had already been crystallized. Practice followed suit, employing, when the spatial solution was complex, a services consultant. Such a practice has, of course, serious shortcomings, namely:
(a) superimposition of services systems on predetermined spatial solutions obviates any chance of a global optimum being achieved for the building as a whole,
(b) while continuing to shoulder full responsibility to the client for the design, the architect is hiving-off what may, in cost terms, amount to over 50% of the job, and
(c) the lack of sound academic courses for services engineers means that few consultants will be versed in design techniques appropriate to strategic decision-making.

The advent of the practising design team, comprising members from a variety of disciplines, including services engineering, represents an attempt to overcome some of the problems associated with the traditional mode of working; there is already evidence, however, that due to differences in education, experience, language and motivation, the difficulties are far from being resolved.

The most recent, and hopeful, signs are coming from a few university schools. Recognizing the need for all members of the design team to have a common educational basis, the concept of 'key-hole man' has been put forward. Figure 7.1 shows 'key-hole man' (continuous line) in relation to the traditional schools' product (broken line): both enclose the same area, but 'key-hole man' has had less 'all-round' education and has specialized in a particular aspect of building design – in this case, services. The idea is that a number of specialist designers is produced, having a common educational base, language and motivation, who together can make an effective and coherent design team. Going hand-in-hand with the specialization, will be a liberalization of the 'core' discipline to include topics such as operational research, decision theory, statistics and design methodology.

A team formed from such a group of design specialists may still have occasion to utilize consultants who are the product of quite different educational structure. The chances of using them effectively, however, will be enhanced due to the specialist knowledge already existing in the team.

Figure 7.1

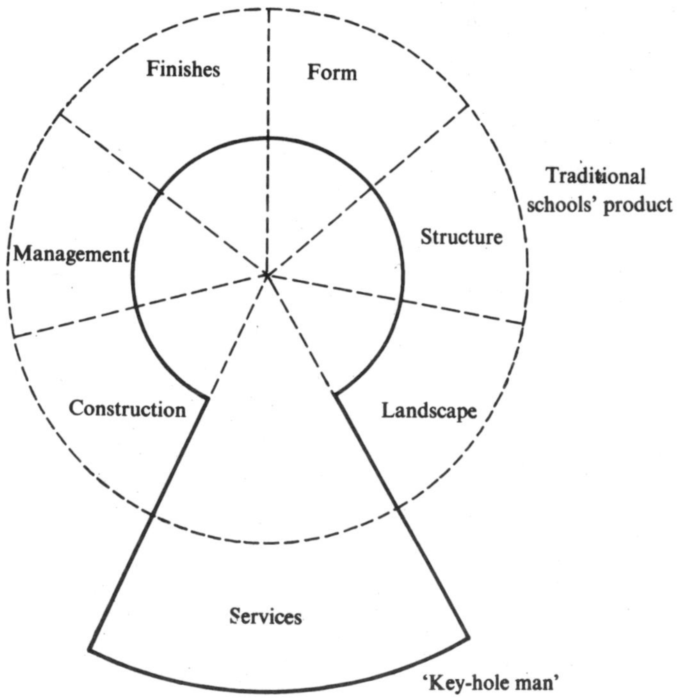

'Key-hole man'

151

It is hoped that this volume will be sufficiently flexible to be of use to schools which continue to produce the generalist practitioner, to schools which offer engineering services as a specialism, and to other educational institutions producing environmental engineers, as such.

Design team working

The procedures described in earlier chapters for the design of service systems are complex; even within the environment of an efficient design team comprising 'key-hole' specialists, the possibility of exploring the interactions of all alternative services design schemata with all the alternative schemata of other systems in the building is extremely low.

In order to limit the area of search for an optimum solution, a hierarchical decision-making structure can be implemented. The Plan of Work incorporated in the Royal Institute of British Architects' *Handbook*[1] identifies hierarchical stages in the design activity on which Markus[2] has built a model of the design activity, which is illustrated in Figure 7.2. The Plan of Work management stages are listed down the left-hand side of the diagram and within each stage the processes of analysis, synthesis, appraisal and decision are identified.

The most likely mode of operation of a design team at each management stage is that of:
(a) analysis of requirements, including statistical ordering and manipulation of data gathered from existing buildings,
(b) the synthesis (or generation) of a design hypothesis, based on the preceding analysis,
(c) the appraisal (or measurement) of the hypothesized solution with regard to cost-in-use and performance on each of a variety of criteria,
(d) modification of the hypothesized solution in the light of the preceding appraisal (represented by the feedback loop in Figure 7.2),
(e) reappraisal,
(f) modification,
(g) reappraisal,
(h) etc.

The process is continued until designer and client are satisfied that the cost/performance balance is the 'optimum' achievable, thus satisfying the design objective function set out in Chapter 1. The role of the services specialist would be analogous to that of the other specialists, i.e., he would conduct analyses of demand data, suggest hypothesized schemes, conduct the cost/performance appraisals relevant to the services, propose modifications to the scheme, etc. In this

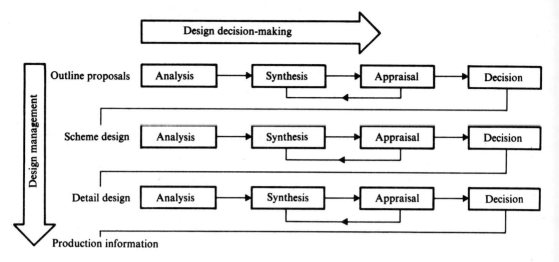

Figure 7.2

way the interactions between the services system and other systems emerge in the iterative process of synthesis and appraisal.

It is of interest to note the parallel between the iterative nature of the design activity as a whole with that of the process set out on pages 120–4 for the design of distribution networks. In both cases the operation of design solutions has been simulated and measurement made of the degree to which operative criteria have been met. The process of simulation promotes not only a convergence on an optimum solution for a particular design problem but also an understanding of the manner in which systems work; as such, it is an ideal method for generating understanding of the disparate, but shared, problems facing design teams.

Technological development

In the opening chapter, mention was made of the fact that in past years engineering systems have taken over many of the functions previously performed by the structure. Whether or not this trend continues will depend on the cost-benefit analysis in any particular case, but it is of interest to conject as to the extent to which service systems could replace structural functions.

As stated in Chapter 1, some of the functions of the window have already been taken over – the functions of providing ventilation (and the associated heating and cooling) and light. The remaining function is that of providing a visual contact with the outside world. An engineering system which could take over this function is closed circuit television. The advantage of closed circuit television is that it affords, if desired, alternative or varying views simply, and could double as an internal communication system. It would be an interesting study to compare the cost-in-use of windows (taking account of heat loss in the winter, solar gain in the summer) and the cost-in-use of closed circuit television.

One of the penalties to be paid for having windows is the ingress of noise from an increasingly noisy external environment. As external and internal spatial boundaries become lighter in mass, the problem of noise increases and some thought is now being given to engineering systems which will improve the acoustic environment. If the problem is one of intelligible sound interference, say from one area of a *Bürolandschaft* office to another, 'white' noise (sometimes referred to as acoustic deodorant) can be introduced through speakers to mask the intelligibility and thus reduce the distraction. A more sophisticated, but as yet less practical approach is to direct an artificially generated sound, having the same intensity and wave length, at the noise source; at the mid-way point between the two neither is audible.

Of course, the most effective way of ensuring a high signal-to-noise ratio in verbal communication is for the correspondents to wear earphones and speak into microphones. Extension of this idea leads to the concept of a 'space-suit' which could give individual control over the thermal, acoustic, visual, olfactory and tactile environments. There is little doubt that such a scheme is technologically feasible – the reader will have his own views on its desirability.

Major technological advances are likely to increase the viability of certain energy conversion plant: work is progressing on fuel cells, direct energy converters, solar heaters, nuclear reactors, thermoelectrical circuits, etc., and those engaged to design buildings which will still be standing in the twenty-first century would do well to keep themselves informed of progress.

Design decision-making

Throughout this book emphasis has been placed on mechanisms for decision-making in the design of engineering services in buildings. The science of decision-making is a rapidly growing one and building designers must keep abreast of methodological developments in this field; even more important, however, is the need, which must be met from within the profession, to develop decision-making techniques specifically relevant to the multi-variate problems of the building industry.

The opportunities offered by the digital computer in the solution of complex building design problems are great, and the profession must not fail to recognize and realize its potential. Applications of the computer to specific aspects of engineering services design have been documented[3,4] and proposals made for appraisal program packages which will integrate decision-making on engineering services design with all other quantifiable aspects of the building.[5]

A final word: engineering services are a major and integral aspect of the building system as a whole, and as such, present the kind of challenge which makes design the most exciting activity to which man can aspire. As with all design endeavour, the need is to be systemic, systematic and imaginative.

Symbols

	Symbol	Meaning
Chapter 2 pp. 16–38	$P; p; q$	probability
	$N; n; r$	number
	$x; y; X$	variable
	f	frequency
	$\bar{x}$	mean value of variable x
	s	standard deviation of variable
	v	probability point of standardized distribution
	r	correlation coefficient
	$a; b$	numerical value
	dm^3	cubic decimetres
	GJ	gigajoules
Chapter 3 pp. 39–64	$\dot{Q}$	rate of heat flow
	A	area; cross-sectional area
	$T; \Delta T$	temperature; temperature difference
	k	thermal conductivity
	$d; l$	measure of distance; length
	K	thermal conductance
	R	thermal resistance
	$\dot{q}$	rate of heat flow through unit area
	h	convection coefficient
	Υ	radiation constant
	ε	emissivity
	F	configuration factor
	U	coefficient of thermal transmittance
	m	mass
	c	specific heat
	t	time
	L	latent heat
	l	latent heat per unit mass
	$n; N$	number
	V	volume
	Q	heat flow
	$a; b$	numerical values
	z	elevation
	v	velocity
	P	pressure

ρ		density
$h; \Delta h$		head loss
$\dot{V}$		rate of volumetric flow
f		friction factor
G		gravitational constant
$x; y$		variables
R		electrical resistance
V		voltage
I		current
W		power
θ		angle
ω		angular frequency
L		inductance
C		capacitance
Z		impedance
ϕ		phase angle
$\cos \phi$		power factor
ρ		resistivity
η		efficiency
p		performance ratio
e		base of natural logarithms
W		watts
kW		kilowatts
J		joules
MJ		megajoules
GJ		gigajoules
$m^2; m^3; dm^3$		square metres; cubic metres; cubic decimetres
kg		kilogrammes
VA		volt-amperes
var		volt-amperes-reactive

Chapter 4 pp. 65–82	i	compound interest rate per annum
	n	number of years
	C_P	present sum of money
	C_F	future sum of money
	C_A	uniform annual payment
	$x; y$	variable
	s	standard deviation
	$\bar{x}$	mean value of the variable x
	P	probability
	C_t	total cost
	C_p	cost of provision
	C_f	cost of failure
	V	voltage
	U	units of electricity (in KWh)
	M	units of electrical maximum demand (in kW)
	K	constant

ϕ	phase angle	
$\cos \phi$	power factor	
p	new pence	
dm^3	cubic decimetres	
V	volts	
VA	volt-amperes	
kVA	kilovolt-ampere	
var	volt-amperes-reactive	
kvar	kilovolt-amperes-reactive	
MJ	megajoules	
kWh	kilowatt-hours (1kWh = 3·6 MJ)	

Chapter 5 pp. 83–129

t	time
p	probability
$n; r$	number
$x; y$	variable
h	pressure head
Δh	head loss
v	velocity
d	diameter
l	length
ρ	density
M	units of electrical maximum demand (in kW)
U	units of electricity (in kWh)
F	configuration factor
$T; \Delta T$	temperature; temperature difference
$\dot{Q}$	heat flow
$\dot{V}$	volumetric flow
c'	specific heat, expressed per unit volume
$\Delta h'$	head loss per unit length
V	volts
kW	kilowatts
°C	degrees Centigrade
MJ	megajoules
mN/m^2	millinewtons per square metre
kg	kilogrammes

Chapter 6 pp. 130–149

W	load
W_H	heating load
W_W	hot water load
W_C	cooling load
W_M	mechanical load
W_I	electrical load
P	plant size
η	efficiency

$x; y; z$	variables
C	cost
c	unit cost
N	number
t	time
l	length
kW/m^2	kilowatts per square metre
GJ/kg	gigajoules per kilogramme
MJ/kg	megajoules per kilogramme

References and further reading

Chapter 1 pp. 7–15

References

1 Markus, T.A. (1967).
The role of building performance,
measurement and appraisal
in design method.
The Architects' Journal. **146.** 1567–
1573.

Further reading

Asimow, M. (1962).
Introduction to design.
New Jersey, Prentice-Hall.

Banham, R. (1969).
*The architecture of the well tem-
pered environment.*
London, Architectural Press.

Broadbent, G.H. (1966).
Design method in architecture.
The Architects' Journal. **144.** 679–
684.

Jones, J.C. & Thornley, D.G.,
eds. (1963).
Conference on design methods.
Oxford, Pergamon Press.

Stone, P.A. (1967).
*Building design evaluation, costs-in-
use.*
London, Spon.

Chapter 2 pp. 16–38

Further reading

Aitchison, J. (1963).
The estimation of design values I.
Building Services Research Unit,
University of Glasgow. Duplicated.

Aitchison, J. & Sculthorpe, D.
(1964).
Design value tables.
Building Services Research Unit,
University of Glasgow. Duplicated.

Bowker, A.H. & Lieberman, G.L.
(1960).
Engineering statistics.
New York, Prentice-Hall.

Carson, W. (1965).
Three simple techniques for
estimating the scale of provision of
service outlets and other facilities
in buildings.
The Architects' Journal. **141.** 585–
590.

Moroney, M.J. (1956).
Facts from figures. 3rd ed.
London, Penguin.

Thomson, J.D. (1970).
*Basic statistical techniques for the
course on engineering services.*
Building Services Research Unit,
University of Glasgow. Duplicated.

Chapter 3 pp. 39–64

References

1 Putnam, P.C. (1953).
Energy in the future.
New York, Van Nostrand.

2 Scientific American. Editorial
Board. (1963).
*Technology and economic develop-
ment.*
London, Penguin.

3 Silver, R.S. (1965).
Fresh water from the sea.
*Proceedings of the Institute of
Mechanical Engineers.* **179.** 135–
153.

Further reading

Billington, N.S. (1967).
Building physics: heat.
Oxford, Pergamon Press.

Brown, H. and others. (1957).
The next hundred years.
London, Weidenfeld and Nicolson.

Cotton, H. (1951).
Applied electricity.
London, Cleaver-Hume Press.

Fisher, J.L. & Potter, N. (1964).
World prospects for natural resources.
Washington, Resources for the Future, Inc.

Henke, R.W. (1966).
Introduction to fluid mechanics.
Reading (Mass.) Addison-Wesley.

Institution of Heating and Ventilating Engineers. (1970).
IHVE Guide.
London.

Thirring, H. (1956).
Power production; the practical application of world energy.
London, Harrap.

Van Straaten, J.F. (1967).
Thermal performance of buildings.
London, Elsevier.

Wylie, J.C. (1959).
The wastes of civilization.
London, Faber and Faber.

Chapter 4   pp. 65–82

References

1 Cissell, R. & Cissell, H. (1969).
Mathematics of finance. 3rd ed.
Boston, Houghton Mifflin.

Further reading

Carson, W. & Maver, T.W. (1966).
Cost-effectiveness and the engineering services in hospitals.
Problems and progress in medical care.
Oxford University Press.
187–205.

Confederation of British Industry. (1966).
Coal: the price structure 1966.
London.

Prest, A.R. & Turvey, R. (1965).
Cost benefit analysis—a survey.
The Economic Journal. **75.** 683–735.

Stone, P.A. (1967).
Building design evaluation, costs-in-use.
London, Spon.

Thomson, J.D. (1968).
Electricity in hospitals.
Building Services Research Unit, University of Glasgow. Duplicated.

Chapter 5   pp. 83–129

References

1 Institution of Heating and Ventilating Engineers. (1970).
IHVE Guide.
London.

2 Ministry of Public Building and Works. (1965).
The building regulations.
London, HMSO.

3 British Standards Institution. (1970).
CP 342: Part 1: Centralized domestic hot water supply. Individual dwellings.
London.

4 British Standards Institution. (1950).
CP3: Engineering and utility services.
London.

5 British Standards Institution. (1952).
CP310: Water supply.
London.

6 Institution of Electrical Engineers. (1966).
Regulations for the electrical equipment of buildings. 14th ed.
London.

Further reading

Billington, N.S. (1967).
Building physics: heat.
Oxford, Pergamon Press.

Faber, O. & Kell, J.R. (1966).
Heating and air conditioning of buildings. 4th ed.
London, The Architectural Press.

Howard, H. (1957).
On pipe sizing accelerated hot-water systems with an electronic digital computer.
Associateship thesis, National College of Heating, Ventilating, Refrigeration and Fan Engineering.

Jay, P. & Hemsley, J. (1968).
Electrical services in buildings.
London, Elsevier.

Jones, A.P. (1967).
Air conditioning engineering.
London, Arnold.

Kinzey, B.Y. & Sharp, H.M. (1963).
Environmental technologies in architecture.
New Jersey, Prentice-Hall.

McGuinness, W.J. and others. (1964).
Mechanical and electrical equipment for buildings. 4th ed.
New York, Wiley.

Maver, T.W. (1966).
Some techniques of operational research illustrated by their application to the problem of hot and cold water plant sizing.
Journal of the Institution of Heating and Ventilating Engineers.
33. 301–313.

Merritt, F.S., ed. (1966).
Mechanical and electrical design of buildings for architects and engineers.
New York, McGraw-Hill.

Sheridan, N.R. and others. (1963).
Air conditioning.
St Lucia, University of Queensland Press.

Thomson, J.D. (1968).
Electricity in hospitals.
Building Services Research Unit, University of Glasgow. Duplicated.

Van Straaten, J.F. (1967).
Thermal performance of buildings.
London, Elsevier.

Further reading

Faber, O. & Kell, J.R. (1966).
Heating and air conditioning of buildings. 4th ed.
London, The Architectural Press.

Heating and Ventilating Research Association. (1965).
District heating: a survey of practice in Europe and America.
London, National Coal Board.

Institution of Heating and Ventilating Engineers. (1970).
IHVE Guide.
London.

Jenkins, N. (1970).
Total energy.
Journal of the Institution of Heating and Ventilating Engineers. **37.**
A26-A29 (Feb.), A34-A36 (March), A34-A41 (April), A17 (May).

Kinzey, B.Y. & Sharp, H.M. (1963).
Environmental technologies in architecture.
New Jersey, Prentice-Hall.

Livingstone, A.H. (1965).
M.A. project report.
Building Services Research Unit, University of Glasgow. Duplicated.

McGuinness, W.J. and others. (1964).
Mechanical and electrical equipment for buildings. 4th ed.
New York, Wiley.

Maver, T.W. (1967).
Energy for hospitals.
Air Conditioning, Heating and Ventilating. **64.** 49–52.

Maver, T.W. & Gratton, B. (1964).
Study of the water and energy services in the hospital as a whole.
Building Services Research Unit, University of Glasgow. Duplicated.

Merritt, F.S., ed. (1966).
Mechanical and electrical design of buildings for architects and engineers.
New York, McGraw-Hill.

Turpin, F.B. (1966).
District heating.
London, Heywood.

What you should know about on-site energy systems. (1964).
Heating, Piping and Air Conditioning. **36.** 160–174.

Chapter 7 pp. 150–155

References

1 Royal Institute of British Architects. (1967).
Handbook of architectural practice and management.
London.

2 Markus, T.A. (1967).
The role of building performance, measurement and appraisal in design method.
The Architects' Journal. **146.** 1567–1573.

3 Ministry of Public Building and Works. (1969).
Bibliography on the application of computers in the construction industry 1962–1967.
London, HMSO.

4 Nevrala, D. and others. (1970).
A comparison of five digital computer programs for calculating maximum air conditioning loads.
Bracknell, Heating and Ventilating Research Association.

5 Maver, T.W. (1970).
A theory of architectural design in which the role of the computer is identified.
Building Science. **4.** 199–207.

Further reading

Asimow, M. (1962).
Introduction to design.
New Jersey, Prentice-Hall.

Broadbent, G.H. (1966).
Design method in architecture.
The Architects' Journal. **144.** 679–684.

Central Statistical Office. (1966).
National income and expenditure.
London, HMSO.

Jones, J.C. & Thornley, D.G., eds. (1963).
Conference on design methods.
Oxford, Pergamon Press.

Stringer, P. (1970).
Architecture as education.
Journal of the Royal Institute of British Architects. **77.** 19–22.

Index